Mrs. Joseph H. Miller

950

2/48

Best wishes
John Dirkenfirst

this

insanity

called

LOVE

this *insanity* called LOVE

John W. Drakeford

WORD BOOKS, *Publisher*

Waco, Texas

London, England

THIS INSANITY CALLED LOVE

Printed in the United States of America
Library of Congress catalog card number: 75–123748

Grateful acknowledgment is made
to Muhlenberg Press
for the use of several quotations
from *Luther on the Christian Home*
by William H. Lazareth
© 1960 Muhlenberg Press

Dedicated to
Eve, May, Jessica, Jess, Doreen and Len
sisters-in-law all,
a bevy of beauty, wit and charm,
who through the years have
increased my appreciation of
this quality called "love"

CONTENTS

Preface

"What is love?"

He would be an extraordinary individual who could come up with some simple answer to this question. On every hand are oversimplified definitions. Something you feel. A way of thinking. A manner of acting. A willingness to sacrifice for others. Taking something you need. A plan of deception. An overwhelming encounter.

Directing a counseling center and conducting conferences have led to questioning and being questioned, answering and being answered. Answering or listening brought an awareness of the utter confusion of thought on this subject.

Living in what has been called the "Age of Love," modern man has little grasp of the concepts said by many to dominate his day and age.

But is this distinctly the dilemma of modern man? The following discussion turns back the pages of history to question a group of people each of whom held a distinctive position concerning love and tries to discover just how they perceived this nebulous idea.

One of the personalities under consideration gives us guidance in just how we should go about the difficult task. Anton

T. Boisen made a unique contribution to theological literature by insisting that students need to supplement their studies of books by examination of the "human document." He claimed that much more could be learned by examining the raw material of our humanity, and observing men and women in both their relationships with, and reactions to, other people.

Just as unusual was the suggestion of an academic psychologist, Dr. Gordon W. Allport, that students of personality might well turn from technical treatises to lighter reading. In all seriousness he advanced the idea that a novelist might give us a view of personality distinctives which may have evaded the more technically-minded and measurement-conscious social scientist.

In an equally upsetting line of thought for the sophisticate, the same Dr. Allport projected the common sense notion that we might ask the subject himself how he saw it all. Allport's erudite writing on research emphasized the "personal document," something produced by the person himself—diary, journal, autobiography, tape recordings—in which he, wittingly or unwittingly, wrote an account of his own inner life.

The work of both the biographer and autobiographer has provided the basic material for this study. Many of these writings are as frank and open as any disclosures made within the walls and confines of a clinic.

The chosen subjects come from widely separated periods of time: Eleanor of Aquitaine, who lived in the twelfth century; Martin Luther, born in 1483; John Wesley, who entered a well populated Epworth rectory in 1703; Benjamin Disraeli, delivered in a wealthy British home in 1804; David Livingstone, whose first cry sounded in a Scottish house in 1813; and Anton T. Boisen, who died in 1966.

They have a bewildering diversity of backgrounds: a queen

who ruled both England and France and exercised a strong sway over the crowned heads of Europe; a miner's son who defined the might of pope and emperor; an itinerant preacher who, seeking only to preach about men's relationship to God, taught a whole society how to live with each other; a prime minister of England in the hour of his country's greatest might; a missionary explorer; and the chaplain of a mental hospital.

Religion played an important part in the experiences of all the major subjects. Eleanor's medieval religion was part of the warp and woof of her culture. Forms, ceremonies, and duties sometimes provided a masquerade behind which political maneuvering took place. In religion's name, a great crusade sent avaricious knights plundering the countryside of distant lands. The princes of the church caused as much travail for Eleanor and her family as did any enemy potentate.

The greatest and most catastrophic upheaval in the history of organized religion provided the background for Martin Luther's improbable marriage. His struggle to break out of the strait jacket of medieval religion had passed its peak when the monk took a nun to wife in the supremely defiant gesture against medieval Catholicism.

John Wesley, the orderly, methodical clerk in holy orders, was caught in a flood tide of spiritual power. Though he belonged to a church that believed in a married clergy, the vision of celibacy ever floated before him. He lived in a constant state of apprehension, fearful lest the love of a woman might pluck him out of the mainstream of God's purposes.

Separated by centuries from Eleanor, Disraeli's religion was, like hers, part of the equipment of political power. Born Jewish, he donned the garments of Christianity as a protection against prejudice; he verbalized an alien faith with facility, periodically using the argument of its Jewish ancestry to squeeze a concession for the people whose features he wore. Unlike Eleanor, the high priestess of courtly love, however, he became the improbable living example of companionate love.

Anton T. Boisen is twentieth-century man. In him is seen the struggle between science and religion. From his bitter personal experience come remarkable insights into the functioning of human personality—and all of it overshadowed by a woman.

What did they all have in common? They all had an experience of one of a variety of human love encounters. An examination of their ups and downs will help to clarify some of the peculiarities of that which we call love.

1

The Medieval Emily Post

ELEANOR OF AQUITAINE (1122–1204)

It might be said a pig caused it all. Had Philip, the eldest son of the king of France, survived, he would have become king, and the second son, Louis Capet, would have followed his natural inclination and training to become a monk. But as Philip, the heir to the French throne, came riding into Paris, a sow aroused from its sleep in a nearby swamp charged into the cavalcade of passing horsemen.

Amid the chaos which followed, the desperate hog darted between the legs of Philip's horse, causing it to stumble and fall. As a result of this injury, Philip lapsed into an unconscious state from which he never recovered.

The younger brother, Louis Capet, was immediately summoned into the presence of his father to be initiated into his

new role as heir to the throne. All thoughts of his cherished
career in the church had to be put aside and preparation made
for him to take up his new princely duties.

Father of these two boys was Louis VI of France, also called
Louis the Fat because of his tremendous bulk. Unable to
climb on the back of a horse or stoop to tie his shoes, his
bodily immobility did not impede the movement of a lively
mind. Those nimble thought processes often contemplated
his vassal Guillaume, the Count of Poitou and Duke of Aquitaine. Guillaume had given his feudal vow of loyalty to the
French king, but he belied with his actions the words which
fell so glibly from his lips.

Poitou and Aquitaine, fair lands in the south of France,
were greater in extent than the French king's own dominions.
Louis had often pondered on his rebellious vassal and the
possibility of forever losing this countryside from his jurisdic-
tion. News of the Duke of Aquitaine's death set him to
thinking and caused him to remember Eleanor, the elder of
the duke's two daughters. Eleanor and Louis Capet—this
match would bind the lands of Poitou and Aquitaine as the
French king's undoubted possession.

Eleanor was not only the heiress of great lands but an
attractive girl besides. Only fifteen years old, she was mature
in mind and attractive in person. Her contemporaries found
her charming and vivacious. The constant journeyings of the
Court of Guillaume around the countryside of southern
France from castle to castle amid the ever changing throng of
courtiers, knights, and troubadours had given her wide social
experience and early brought her a degree of sophistication
rarely found in a fifteen-year-old.

There is every evidence to show that Eleanor at fifteen was
considerably more mature than the seventeen-year-old prince
to whom her marriage was being planned by the king.

When it came to marrying, a medieval woman knew that

hers was not to reason why. Marriage fulfilled the important political function of binding estates and perpetuating names, and she knew she must accept her destiny. Louis Capet rejoiced at the prospect of such a bride. Eleanor may not have been delighted in such great degree, but she realized where the path of duty lay; as the prince rode in to the castle with his glittering escort of noblemen, she made preparation for the wedding celebration.

The nuptial ceremonies took place in the historic church of Saint André. Having made their confession, the prince and the duchess exchanged vows in the presence of surrounding nobility, with Geoffrey, the Archbishop of Bordeaux, officiating. The day reached its climax with a great wedding feast terminated only with the departure of the bride and groom for their future home in Paris.

Along the way the young prince received the news that his father, Louis the Fat, had passed from this world. The domains of France and Aquitaine had been welded in the nick of time.

The coronation which followed their arrival in Paris made Louis the king and Eleanor the queen of France.

Because of his youthfulness, the king returned to his studies and followed his interests in his religious exercises. The high-spirited Eleanor, accustomed to the multitudinous social activities of the courts of Poitou and Aquitaine, found Parisian life rather dull, especially her serious minded husband. She lamented, "I thought to have married a king but find I am wed to a monk."

I

Nobody watched the marriage and accession of Queen Eleanor with more apprehension than did Bernard, Abbot of Clairvaux. In his complex personality were brought together many of the conflicting ideas of his day. A strange mixture of mysticism and activism, while professing to long for monastic solitude, he periodically donned his white cassock and ventured forth from the monastery to correct heresy, or to rebuke rulers lax in their allegiance to their holy father the pope. It was small wonder his contemporaries referred to him as the "hawk of Rome."

Eleanor's forebears and relatives had not always been dutiful sons and daughters of the Church. Her father, Guillaume, had been a thorn in the side of many a church father. Opposing the pope over the appointment of bishops in his domains, his intransigence was so overt that the church excommunicated him with bell, book, and candle.

Guillaume showed such scant regard for this dire penalty that he reacted by launching himself upon a crusade against the clergy. The duke proved to be such a formidable antagonist that the embattled clergy in their hour of need sent out an appeal for help to Bernard of Clairvaux.

The redoubtable duke, not one whit dismayed by the advent of the Hawk of Rome, determined to beard him in his den. Riding up to the church where Bernard was saying mass, he waited for the exit of the abbot. Bernard, having heard the news of the duke's arrival, took the initiative, seized hold of the pyx, a heavy box supposed to contain the body of Christ, and rushed down the aisle to brandish the formidable weapon in front of Guillaume's eyes, all the while demanding that he abandon his sinful ways.

Surprised by the rapid turn of events, Guillaume fell to the floor in some kind of a fit and lay there groaning. It was all over in a moment. Bernard was victor. The Church resumed its authority.

After four years of marriage to Eleanor, King Philip, the former obedient son of the Church, began to act rebelliously and offensively toward the Body of Christ. There was no doubt in Bernard's mind as to where the difficulty lay. He had already been pouring out thinly veiled denunciations of Eleanor and her companions for their frivolity and the worldly apparel they were accustomed to wear.

Louis kicked over the traces with a vengeance. He quarrelled with the pope over the appointment of the Bishop of Bourges. When the pope sent a letter to the royal court in which he accused the King of France of behaving "like a foolish schoolboy," Louis really took umbrage. To satisfy his tender conscience and give him a heavenly sanction for his behavior, the king made a vow on holy relics that he would never let the papal appointee take his place in the cathedral at Bourges.

Then there was Petronilla, the younger sister of Eleanor. Anxious for Petronilla's marriage, Eleanor had found the king's eldest cousin ready and willing to espouse the young lady. The chief difficulty lay in a previous marriage. Working behind the scenes, Eleanor encouraged Louis to find three bishops, who under royal pressure ascertained that the first marriage was not according to the laws of the church, annulled the union, and united the nobleman to Petronilla.

The news of these doings aroused the ire of Bernard, who immediately dispatched a messenger to the pope. In a remarkably short time, considering the distance and difficulty of communication, there came a papal edict condemning the clergy who had participated in the annulment and marriage. By papal decree Eleanor's sister was no longer the wife of the man with whom she lived.

Driven on by some streak of obstinacy, Louis attacked the Count of Champagne, who had opposed both Louis' ecclesiastical appointments and the marriage of Petronilla. The royal armies pillaged the countryside. In one unfortunate incident they gave a town to the flames and over a thousand people died in the conflagration.

Bernard addressed himself to the king in a letter of rebuke and warning that displayed some of the abbot's apprehensions, ". . . from whom except the devil can I say this counsel proceeds. . . . Do not, my king, with rash audacity lift your hand against the terrible Lord who takes away the breath of kings. I speak sharply, because I fear sharp things for you." [1]

The monkish Louis' interest in the war began to subside. The cries of those innocent people rang in his ears. He fell into a state of depression. His troops were withdrawn. He confessed his sin, recanted and flew into the arms of the Church. But even though his relationship with Rome was regularized it helped him little.

Eleanor had not been far from his side in all of these experiences and although he loved her with what a contemporary has called "foolish fondness," she could do little to shake his depression. His advisers feared for his life.

At long last came a confrontation between Eleanor and Bernard. The Abbot of Clairvaux urged the queen to help in the spiritual restoration of the king and held promise of the consolations of the Church which might be hers if she too were truly penitent.

The lady showed no interest in the subject under discussion. She had one consuming concern, that the marriage of her sister, the Lady Petronilla, should be regularized. With true feminine skill for argumentation, she proceeded to marshal a whole series of arguments to show the marriage was legitimate and that the pope had made a grave error by casting any shadow of doubt upon it.

No longer was there a vestige of doubt in Bernard's mind: Eleanor was the evil genius leading the king on his downward pathway to perdition—a true daughter of Eve, the temptress of man. Filled with righteous indignation, Bernard warned Eleanor, "Put an end to your interference in the affairs of state."

A later meeting followed with Eleanor in the role of a penitent, but again the unexpected happened. In a subdued note she pointed out to Bernard that she had been married seven years. Now twenty-two years old, she had still not presented the king with an heir. Could the Abbot of Clairvaux implore heaven that she might be granted the boon of a son? Pleased with her more docile attitude, Bernard promised intercession to the Virgin on her behalf.

In due time Eleanor delivered her child, not a son, but a daughter. The infant was named Marie in gratitude for the goodness of the Queen of Heaven.

II

In his search for alleviation from guilt, Louis had considered the possibility of a pilgrimage. There had been moments before when the pious king had seen himself, palm in hand, visiting the scenes of our Lord's earthly ministry. The thought of these precious lands now overrun by the infidel fostered the pious hope that he might be the instrument in God's hand to release the Holy Land from the Saracen.

Of course Eleanor was behind it. Eight years of life in the French court had left her bored and dissatisfied. Her uncle, Raymond of Antioch, had kept up his stream of gifts, emissaries, and now appeals for help in the difficulties he faced in the historic city of Antioch where he presently ruled. Eleanor easily fanned the flame in the pious Louis' heart. The king communicated to the pope in Rome his hopes of leading an expedition to free Palestine. The pope gave an encouraging reply.

Facing schism and faction, and living in exile, the idea of a crusade appealed to Pope Eugenius. Might not a mighty crusade serve to unite a divided Christendom? In his dilemma the pope turned to Rome's Hawk, Bernard of Clairvaux, and gave to him the responsibility for preaching and planning the crusade.

So they launched the most futile of all enterprises, a military campaign in the name of the Prince of Peace. The most improbable combination, Queen Eleanor and Bernard of Clairvaux, ramrodded the venture. Eleanor worked behind the scenes prodding and cajoling the laggards while Bernard preached with great effectiveness to enlist large numbers of recruits for the enterprise.

No more significant evidence of Eleanor's influence could be found than the great numbers of women bent on joining the crusade. These ladies of noble birth dressed in white were known as the Amazons. They made a truly remarkable sight as they moved in the midst of the horde of Frenchmen traveling across Europe on their venture characterized by lofty objectives and poor behavior.

As a faithful shepherd, King Louis brought up in the rear of the procession. Eleanor and her Amazons moved in the midst, sometimes mounted on their horses, or drawn in wains, or carried on litters. They spent their evenings in elaborate tents and finally drifted off to sleep in their painted beds. Musicians helped them while away the tedious hours in an atmosphere that was as luxurious as that of King Louis' camp was austere.

Local populations who had witnessed a previous crusade lived in mortal fear of the pillaging crusaders, while their rulers plotted and planned to use the visitors for their own selfish ends. As often as it could be managed, the crusaders were steered away from the cities, sold food and supplies at exorbitant prices, and frequently misdirected into pathways that best suited the ends of the local rulers.

In one disastrous episode Eleanor's vassal Geoffrey de Rancom—and it was believed at her express wish—disobeyed orders as to where to camp for the night. Instead of the easily defended but bleak tableland, he led the way to the lush but more vulnerable valley below. The shroud of night settled over the camp, providing cover for the Turks who charged in on their scrubby ponies to launch a surprise attack that brought chaos and carnage to the French ranks. Hundreds of the flower of French soldiery left their bleaching bones scattered across the countryside. Eleanor's vassal was ignominiously dismissed and her influence greatly diminished.

Discouraged at their poor progress on the land route, the noblemen embarked on Greek ships at Satalia, setting sail for Antioch. They left behind them seven thousand foot soldiers who were forever lost to the Louis' crusade when they were most needed.

Not only were they lost to Louis. Fearful of the French, the Greek allies at Satalia refused them admission to the inner city. An awful pestilence spread in their ranks causing them to flee into the arms of the encircling Turks. The infidels, overwhelmed by the pathetic sight of their enemies, received them graciously, and the French infantry was absorbed into the life of the very people they had come to destroy.

After disaster, hunger, and hardship, Eleanor's Uncle Raymond opened his arms in welcome in the city of Antioch. It was not exactly with an unselfish interest, for Raymond saw the French king as bringing reinforcements for his military campaigns and the expansion he had planned as a means of adding strength to the borders of his own kingdom.

Eleanor spent long hours in conversation with her uncle—too many, malicious tongues said. There were questions over the propriety of the relationship. Eleanor championed Raymond's cause and tried to convince her husband that the purposes of the crusade could be served by joining in Raymond's enterprise. After the bleakness of Philip's court, Eleanor felt quite at home with her uncle and his courtiers from her native south of France. She was willing to settle here and enjoy the creature comforts of her uncle's castle while Louis and his men battled the infidel.

Louis dug in his heels. It must be Jerusalem. Not just to extend Raymond's boundaries had he come so far. For once Eleanor could not sway him. In her frustration she defiantly threw down the gauntlet. Louis might go on to Jerusalem but he could go alone. She'd had enough. She would settle in Antioch. This would be her home.

Eleanor dramatically announced to Louis that their marriage was at an end. With that feminine memory that often frustrates men, Eleanor recalled that it was none other than Bernard who had suggested that her marriage to the king was consanguineous. It finally came out that when Bernard was rebuking Louis he had said, "How is it that the king is so scrupulous about consanguinity in the case of Thibault's heirs, when everyone knows that he himself has married his cousin in the fourth degree?" [2]

Reasoning with that frustrating feminine logic, Eleanor now concluded Bernard had condemned the marriage between her and Louis. The slow-witted and devout Louis had a difficult time answering this argument.

With the news of Louis' decision to move on to Jerusalem, Raymond flew into one of his celebrated towering rages. His hospitality was at an end. If Louis was not going to lend his support to extending the boundaries of Antioch, he had better depart without delay.

In contrast with their triumphal entry, Louis' greatly diminished French expeditionary force moved out of Antioch in the early morning hour. In the middle, and surrounded by a heavy guard, went an unwilling Eleanor. Louis was through with his gentle handling of the woman who had manipulated and maneuvered him for so long. He insisted that this time she was going to do it his way.

The Second Crusade failed miserably. Remnants of the mighty army came struggling back to France. Louis and Eleanor visited the sacred spots of Palestine. The military accomplishments were nil.

The relationship between Eleanor and Louis remained strained. The king was as devoted as ever; Eleanor, sulking and sour. Even a visit to the pope resulted in little more than a temporary reconciliation. Eleanor had become pregnant. For a moment there was a fluttering hope; then she gave birth to a daughter.

III

Eleanor finally obtained what has sometimes been called "the greatest divorce in history," on the convenient grounds of consanguinity. The Archbishop of Sens declared the marriage dissolved, the children legitimate and both parties free to marry again.

Following the dissolution of the marriage, Eleanor set out for her ancestral home in Poitiers. Word of her new status spread, and she became fair game for any feudal lord who could detain her. Geoffrey of Anjou made an attempt to waylay her and failed. As she neared a crossing of the river Loire, a warning came of Thibault of Blois waiting at the ford. She evaded him by taking another route.

Arriving at her castle in Poitiers, Eleanor had scarcely caught her breath when Henry, called Plantagenet, because of the sprig of broom he wore in his bonnet, came to woo her. Eleanor was nearly thirty years of age, and Henry, then eighteen years old, was described by a contemporary as "heavy, bull-necked, sensual, with a square jaw, freckled face, reddish hair, and fiery eyes that blazed in sudden paroxysms of anger . . . a rough, passionate, uneasy young man." Within eight weeks of her divorce by Louis, her ex-husband was horrified to hear that Eleanor had become Henry's wife and Duchess of Normandy.

By an unusual set of circumstances, the year 1154 saw Henry Plantagenet crowned Henry II of England, thus making Eleanor a queen for the second time in her life.

After the painful years in the French court with her monkish husband, Eleanor must have responded to the invigorating leadership of Henry. Determined to bring about law and order, Henry became a king in presence and activity as well as in fact. The royal household, numbering up to two hundred, was constantly on the move, enabling Eleanor to become familiar with her new British kingdom.

It was a pace too great for even an activist like Henry to maintain. Into his life came the wordly-minded Thomas Becket to whom he gave the position of chancellor. This genius of organization became the model loyal public servant. In what must have seemed to him a master stroke of diplomacy, Henry then appointed Becket as Archbishop of Canterbury.

The change from a worldly-minded, self-indulgent follower of the king to a devoted humble servant of the church created a drama which reached its dénouement with the martyrdom of Becket. That single event dogged Henry's pathway through all his days.

The new dominions of Henry and the older lands where

Eleanor was born and nurtured were separated by the English Channel. Frequently she made that journey to spend more than half her time in the French lands of her childhood. She never forgot she was the Countess of Poitou and the Duchess of Aquitaine. These titles she valued far more highly than that of Queen of England.

With a fertility that must have annoyed and frustrated her ex-husband, the king of France, Eleanor produced a large family. Five sons and three daughters were added to the two daughters she had borne by the French king.

Two strong-minded people like Eleanor and Henry were bound to have trouble. Passing years witnessed a deterioration in their relationship. The king, with a wandering eye for a pretty girl, was apparently not all that a husband might be. Eleanor compensated by increasingly giving herself to the concerns of her children, who in rapid succession were destined to occupy positions of power in the royal houses of Europe.

IV

On the domestic front Henry was not too successful. He kept an estranged Eleanor a virtual prisoner in her castle for sixteen weary years. Nevertheless she exercised strong influence over her children. A fresco painted on the wall of Henry's Winchester castle symbolized the family relationships. The work of art showed a great eagle being attacked by four eaglets. Henry saw himself as the eagle and the eaglets as his four turbulent sons. (One son had died in 1156.) If the artist had added a female eagle in the corner signaling the eaglets, Eleanor's role in the family drama would have been more adequately portrayed.

The eventide of Henry's life saw a full scale attack by the eaglets. During Henry's last campaign in France, Richard, in his father's presence, gave allegiance to the French king.

As he lay dying in his castle, Henry called for Roger Malchael to read the list of his nobles who had defected. To his horror the king discovered that John's name led the rest, and he cried, "Is it true that John, whom I loved beyond all my sons and for whose gain I suffered all this misery, has forsaken me?" [3] He turned his face to the wall in the lonely misery which could only be alleviated by death.

Richard the Lion-Hearted, born in England, educated in Poitiers in the tradition of the Court of Love, was in every way his mother's son. He was a gifted troubadour, composer, military engineer, leader and general, and after his father's death his accession to the throne gave him the title of King of England. But being a king was secondary to his romantic crusading ventures.

The first five months of Richard's reign were spent in raising money to finance a crusade, upon which he embarked, leaving the redoubtable Eleanor to govern England as regent. Captured and imprisoned on his way back from Palestine, his ransom of 150,000 marks was double the annual income of the British crown. But this amount was extorted from the English people. Shortly after his release he became involved in conflict in France where he was killed by an archer's arrow while fighting over a cache of gold.

Richard's brother John, known as Lackland because he had been given no territory as a son of the king, was one of the most miserable monarchs ever to wear the British crown. The struggle of free men against tyranny has seldom been more dramatically portrayed than in the exploits of Robin Hood and his Merry Men as they defied the rule of John and his minions. But even in these stories there is a Maid Marion of noble birth who moves like an angel amongst the adoring rebels.

John's negative contribution was the despotic spirit which caused the nobles to revolt and compel him to sign Magna Charta at Runnymede. Thus democracy gained a foothold by establishing the writ of habeas corpus, trial by jury, the embryonic principle of no taxation without representation, and a firm limitation upon the monarchy.

V

Eleanor had the aura of romance about her. Wife of two kings, she was the mother of two more in the persons of her sons, Richard the Lion-hearted and John Lackland. Two of her daughters ascended to the throne—Eleanor of Castile and Joanne, Queen of Sicily.

In many ways Eleanor's was a restless and rugged life in a crude and difficult period of history. When her son Richard the Lion-hearted was captured and imprisoned in Austria as he was returning from his crusade, she not only worked unceasingly to raise the high ransom, but undertook the journey across the continent to negotiate his release.

Eleanor's place in history, however, is not assured by her heroic masculine exploits, but rather by the romantic interlude of the years she spent at Poitiers where she popularized the notions of gentleness, courtesy and compassion. Living in her castle, she gathered around her a court thronging with poets, philosophers, clerics and knights. Her daughter by the king of France, Marie, the Countess of Champagne, who had been wooed by Henry before he took her mother to wife, joined forces with Eleanor, and by their united efforts they developed the Court of Love.

The Court of Love was fashioned on the legal pattern of the

feudal system. Gathered in a newly constructed hall in the castle of Poitiers, with freshly cut rushes strewn on the floor, the knights and courtiers sat on the stone benches around the wall and awaited the arrival of Eleanor, Marie, and their jury. The women entered, sometimes as many as sixty of them, elegantly clothed in garments made of "rich and previous stuff," and took their places on the daïs. Following the preliminaries, an advocate representing an anonymous petitioner approached the platform and presented a question of the dilemma of heart of a certain knight or lady. After hearing the facts, Eleanor and her jury deliberated on the problem and delivered their verdict.

In the course of arriving at these verdicts, relationships of men and women were discussed, personified, and magnified, and the decisions reached were recorded. Troubadours went out to praise the decisions of the court:

> God save Lady Eleanor
> Queen who art the arbiter
> Of honor, wit and beauty,
> Of largesse and loyalty.

The fifty-two-year-old Eleanor, presiding over the Court of Love, must have felt more than a bit flattered when news came of the troubadours singing

> The sweet young queen
> Draws the thoughts of all upon her
> As sirens lure the witless mariners
> Upon the reefs.

It was probably all the more sustaining as news came of husband Henry's rather liberal interpretation of his marriage vows and the stories of his affairs.

One persistently recorded story tells that Eleanor had her own lover, the poet Bernard, who poured out his verses in

Eleanor's honor. The details are lacking, but in the spirit of courtly love Eleanor the beloved was of exalted station, sometimes encouraging and at other times rejecting, but always keeping her lover in a state of frustrated anticipation. A summons from King Henry took Bernard to England and cold reality.

Following the custom of the Middle Ages, religion was an integral part of the process, and the cleric André, Marie's chaplain, wrote a manual called *Treatise on Love and Its Remedy* in which the devious practices of love-making were set out. Of particular interest are André's *Rules of Love*. A sampling of the thirty-one rules includes:

    I. Marriage is not a proper excuse for abstaining from loving.
    II. He who is not jealous cannot love.
    III. No one may be constrained by love for two.
    XIII. Love that has become promiscuous has rarely been able to endure.
    XIV. Easy acquisition renders love contemptible; difficult acquisition makes it precious to have.
    XV. All lovers have been wont to grow pale in the presence of the loved one.
    XIX. If love lessens, it wanes soon and rarely recovers.
    XXI. The emotion of love always grows from true jealousy.
    XXIII. One preoccupied with love eats and sleeps less.
    XXVII. The lover cannot have enough of the loved one.

A reading of these rules highlights many of the peculiarities of courtly love. Kelly says André based his literary effort on Ovid's Latin treatises on *The Art of Loving* and *The Remedy of Love*, but with an essential difference. In Ovid's writings man is the master, employing his arts to seduce the woman for his pleasure, while in André's writings, the woman is the mistress, with the man her pupil.[4]

In courtly love the process of courtship is closely defined and stylized, progressing in four distinct stages. The first stage was that in which the lover was an *aspirant* worshiping from a distance. He then became a *supplicant* as he summoned courage to assert his love. From this he moved to being a *recognized suitor*, and the lady permitted him to pay court and dedicate his songs to her. As a final step he became an *accepted lover*. The demands made of the man of humility, patience, and courtesy in the service of women were a long way from the generally accepted traditional ideas of the feminine sex.

Eleanor's reign in Poitiers reached its pinnacle in the years 1170–1174 when it was rudely interrupted by the call of Henry to join him in England. There is evidence to show that many of the noblemen of that day objected to the feminine prominence in the Court of Love, and after her departure for England, Eleanor's influence waned somewhat in the decisions of the Court of Love.

Eleanor, called by some "the greatest Frenchwoman," finished out her days in the home of her childhood. Her turbulent life drew to a close amidst the terrifying news of war within her territory. At 83 years of age she passed from this world. The sound of warfare and the crash from the demolition of castles and fortresses may have symbolized the devastating effects of the formulations of Courtly Love upon many of the time-honored institutions of man.

2

The Monk Who Married a Nun

MARTIN LUTHER (1483–1546)

To say the least, the proposal was unusual. Dr. Amsdorf brought a message from Katherine von Bora to Dr. Martin Luther. Time was fleeting. She was twenty-six years old, an advanced age for an unmarried girl in that day. In her own mind she had finally decided she would not marry Dr. Glatz, the second choice of Dr. Martin for her. She now reached the conclusion she would either marry Dr. Amsdorf, a visitor to Wittenberg and bearer of the message or . . . maybe Dr. Luther . . . .

Katherine was the last of a group of women Luther had on his hands. The expanding reformation movement had seen many monks leaving their monasteries, and nuns soon followed suit. A group of these women sent a message requesting

Luther's help, and he in turn enlisted the aid of the sixty-year-old Leonard Koppe, a highly respected merchant who periodically delivered barrels of herring to the convent. The nuns were surreptitiously bundled into the merchant's wagon, giving the impression he was merely carrying off nine empty herring barrels. Out the gates of the convent they passed to freedom and a new life.

Gaining liberty was one thing; knowing where to go was another. Having helped the women escape, Luther now had to decide what to do with his ex-nuns. To find husbands for them offered a rather obvious possibility, and the ladies were willing. One by one they married until two years after their escape only one still remained. Her name: Katherine von Bora.

The unmarried ex-nun had been born in 1499 into a noble house. With the full consent of her father and stepmother, she entered the convent school and continued until her fifteenth year. After her novitiate she became a nun at the tender age of sixteen. Now, eight years later, the twenty-four-year-old Katherine was starting a new life.

To her convent-induced shyness was added an aloof manner which kept her from making friends easily. Fortunately for her Philip and Margaret Reichenbach, a newly married couple, gave her the opportunity to go into their home. A promising young lawyer, Philip had a large house to which to take his new bride.

With the same zeal she had formerly applied to her religious calling, Katherine gave herself to mastering domestic skills. So well did she do them that Margaret nicknamed her a "model of industry." However, despite her application and success in household skills, she missed two opportunities for wedded bliss.

When Jerome Baumgartner, of noble birth and a student of

law, came from his native Nuremberg to visit Wittenberg in 1523, Katherine attracted him; and she in turn responded to his overtures of love. Without being formally engaged, they nevertheless reached an understanding. Jerome departed for home to tell his parents the good news, leaving Katherine to await his return and the happy wedding day.

The days lengthened into weeks with never a word from the distant lover. Apparently his noble parents did not take kindly to the idea of their son and heir marrying an apostate nun, and he couldn't bring himself to break the sad tidings to his fiancée. Katherine's concern mounted with the passing days until at last she sought the help of Luther.

With customary compassion for those in difficulty, the reformer wrote the young man seeking to discover his intentions, "If you want your Katie von Bora, you had best act quickly before she is given to someone else who wants her. She has not yet conquered her love for you. I would gladly see you married to each other." [1] It was a gentle urging, with enough threat of competition to stimulate a flagging interest.

To this fatherly request there came no reply. Then followed the whispered story that Jerome was planning to marry a fourteen-year-old girl, Sybilla Dichtl. The news plunged Katherine into depression.

Luther had mentioned "someone else" in his letter. This second suitor was not nearly so eligible as Jerome. Luther had in mind Dr. Kasper Glatz, onetime rector of Wittenberg University. To Katherine he was as objectionable as Jerome had been desirable. She would not have him at any price.

Martin, now forty-two years of age, was not really open to the suggestion of marriage. To the earlier news that monks were marrying, Luther had responded, "Good heavens! They won't give me a wife." Katherine's gentle hint itself may have been made in jest, and it seems Luther accepted it in this vein.

On a visit to his father, he jokingly related the proposal of Katherine. His father took the suggestion seriously and reminded Martin that as the only living son there rested upon him the responsibility for carrying on the family name. So came the decision to marry.

Was this the hidden motive behind Luther's quarrel with the Roman church? Could it be that all his theologizing was simply an elaborate cover-up of his sexual needs? Henry VIII, King of England, had written against the heresy of Martin Luther with such persuasion and conviction that the pope bestowed on him the title "Defender of the Faith," a title used by his Protestant successors to this very day. Yet Henry found it fairly easy to relinquish his championship of Roman Catholicism and to insist on reforming the English church when he wanted to divorce an unwanted wife. Sexual impulse easily overcame religious conviction.

Men are made in no uniform mold. Nowhere is this more clearly seen than in the complexity and variety of human sexuality. Luther pondered the problem and seemed puzzled as to why some men had so many difficulties with sexual impulses. Reading of the early church fathers, he wondered aloud at the intensity of their struggles with sexual temptation:

Even as an old man, St. Augustine still complained of having [nocturnal] pollutions. St. Jerome beat his chest with a stone in vain because of his powerful temptations. Yet he could not overcome the evil or drive out his inward desires for a dancing girl he once saw in Rome. St. Francis, the barefoot monk, made figures out of snow and then caressed them in order to quiet the lust which burned within him. St. Benedict threw himself into the midst of thorny bushes as a sexual remedy. Whenever he was overcome by evil lust, he stripped himself naked and crawled through thorny bushes to lacerate his body. St. Bernard pommeled himself so badly that his body just reeked and stank and nobody could remain near him. . . . I am amazed that the holy fathers permitted themselves to be plagued with such childish temptations—rather than the higher spiritual assaults—since they held such high offices as rulers of the church.[2]

None of their experiences seem to have evoked a response in Luther. He acknowledged he was "not a sexless stone" but sexual frustration doesn't seem to have been a vitally important issue for him. A recent psychoanalytic investigator whose eagle eye would have been the first to really discern such a reaction has reached the conclusion that sex was not really crucial in Luther's experience.

It is also noteworthy that Luther made his final break with the Roman church in 1521, but it was not until four years later, in 1525, that he made the decision to marry—hardly the impulsive action of a sex-starved monk. There is no real reason to doubt Luther's own evaluation of the place of his marriage, "God knows that I never expected to go as far as I did. I thought only of attacking indulgences. Had anyone at Worms told me that in six years I would marry, and then sit at home and father three sons, I would never have believed him."[3]

The marriage was neither the infatuation of youth nor the fantasy of middle age. The romantic love movement in southern France had not influenced Luther. He had earlier let it be known that of the band of nine fugitive nuns, he was really attracted to Eva von Schönfeld and found the proud and haughty Katie too distant.

Martin was later able to say, "I am not infatuated though I cherish my wife." He gave three reasons for his marriage: to please his father, to spite the pope and the devil, and to seal the witness of his martyrdom. He was kind enough not to mention the plight of Katherine.

Seldom has a marriage aroused more controversy and criticism from both enemy and friend. Opponents in the Catholic

church raised a chorus of protest. The "Defender of the
Faith," Henry VIII of England (and who was more qualified
in the area of man-woman relationships?) complained about
Luther's "immoral" behavior. Erasmus in one of his sorriest
moments helped spread a rumor that Martin was forced to
marry Katherine because she had borne him a child. The
biggest blow of all was from his co-worker Philip Melanch-
thon. Ever melancholy, Philip now lamented the sad mistake of his friend.

I

It is often said that a bachelor over thirty years old is so set
in his ways as to be a poor marriage risk. Martin in his
forty-third year found his flexibility tested and tried. He said,
"Before I married, the bed was not made for a whole year and
became foul with sweat. But I worked so hard and was so
weary I tumbled in without noticing it." [4] In his own quaint
manner he mentioned other differences, "There is a lot to get
used to in the first year of marriage; one awakes in the morning and finds a pair of pigtails which were not there before."

Katie's wishes had to be heeded. Martin planned to attend
his friend Spalatin's wedding, but Katherine, fearful of what
might happen, urged him not to go. It has been said there are
women who run the house by water power; Katherine, like
Delilah of old, cried until he finally changed his mind.

Like so many other aspects of this marriage, the honeymoon
was somewhat unorthodox. No sooner were the rather prolonged wedding celebrations concluded and the host of well-
wishers on their way than there came a hammering on the
door. It was Andreas Carlstadt, who by his extreme attitudes
had embarrassed Luther and finally precipitated a break between them. Carlstadt, in trouble again and fleeing for his life,

turned to the alienated Luther to receive an undeserved welcome. So began the first night of married life for Katherine and Martin, setting the pattern of generous hospitality for the years to follow.

Many a promising marriage is wrecked upon the shoals of finances, and it is sometimes suggested the wedding vows might be altered to read, "till debt us do part." Luther at forty-two had no financial assets. He took no profits from his books and had never been able to save money. Fiscal responsibility was not the reformer's outstanding virtue. What little money came his way slipped lightly through his fingers. His wife soon discovered that she had to be treasurer and keep a tight grip on the domestic finances.

In a masterpiece of understatement, Luther said on one occasion, "I do not believe I can be accused of niggardliness." Their banker soon learned not to honor a draft from Luther unless Katherine first approved it. She had her hands full. Martin's irresponsibility is shown in his statement, "I do not worry about debts because when Katie pays for one another one comes." A letter to a friend shows how far this wifely care had to go. "I am sending you a vase as a wedding present. P.S. Katie's hid it."

In many ways the product of his peasant childhood, Luther loved the soil and took care of the garden, growing cucumbers, beans, melons, and a host of vegetables. But he didn't toil alone. The industrious and diligent Katie carried on the lion's share of the work, tended the orchard, kept a fishpond, cared for the barnyard and did her own slaughtering.

The visitor on the honeymoon might have been an augury of things to come. They lived in an old cloister with rooms either too large or too small. The plastering remained uncompleted. What had been the library and dining room would easily accommodate upwards of fifty people while the rest of the rooms were individual cells. Katie brought an aunt to help with the housework, and other relatives drifted in to swell the ever-increasing household.

In her struggle to cope with financial problems, Katie took in students as boarders. She hoped they would help with the expenses and also stimulate Martin's constantly active mind. So came an invading hoard of curious young men, giving the Luthers a family group which fluctuated between twenty and thirty. Each student occupied an individual cell. The hope was that their presence would be stimulating for Martin; financially there was little advantage. The kindly disposed Luther allowed the nonpayers to eat up the profits of the regular contributors.

In rapid succession came other mouths to be fed. Luther fathered a family of six, three sons and three daughters. His first-born, Hans, was his pride and joy. Beaming down in satisfaction he complimented himself for having given up the monk's vow for the joys of family life. He addressed himself to his squirming child, "Kick away, son. The pope tied me in diapers too, but I kicked them off."

II

The family meal has become the focal point for some sociologists who see it as the center around which many of the family rituals develop. Meal table conversations have taken on a new significance. One authority claims the most important single factor in determining a child's philosophy of life is what is talked about at the meal table. If this be really so, Luther's children must have been privileged above all others.

The reformer sat for meals surrounded by student boarders who felt that this offered a golden opportunity for furthering their education. Gathered around the festive board, they not only consumed the food so industriously and painstakingly garnered and prepared by Katie, but seized every crumb of wisdom that fell from their teacher's lips. Some sat with notebooks at their elbows ready to record every word.

The students' behavior scandalized Katherine. Painfully conscious of a constant struggle to balance the budget, she maintained they should make a financial contribution for their educational privileges. Some of them not only failed to pay for their board or instruction, but actually made money for themselves by recording and classifying their teacher's conversations and publishing them in books. The most outstanding of these efforts came to be known as Luther's *Table Talk*.

Luther sometimes objected to the student activity, but the ham in him prevented a move to stop it. He talked on an infinite variety of subjects and his remarks "ranged from the ineffable majesty of God the Omnipotent to the frogs in the Elbe. Pigs, popes, pregnancies, politics and proverbs jostle one another." [5] There are some 6,596 entries of Luther's sayings in these collections. Some deal with family life as is seen in the following extracts.

The monks are the fleas on Almighty's fur coat.

When asked why he was so violent, Luther replied, "A twig can be cut with a bread knife, but an oak calls for an ax."

God uses lust to impel men to marriage, ambition to office, avarice to earning, and fear to faith.

Maternity is a glorious thing, since all mankind have been conceived, borne, and nourished of women. All human laws should encourage the multiplication of families.

Men have broad and large chests, and small narrow hips, and more understanding than women, who have but small and narrow breasts, and broad hips, to the end they should remain at home, sit still, keep house, and bear and bring up children.

The reproduction of mankind is a great marvel and mystery. Had God consulted me in the matter, I should have advised him to continue the generation of the species by fashioning them of clay in the way Adam was fashioned.

Many a modern mortal has worried about the invasion of his personal privacy. Reports about the proliferation of ingenious electronic snooping devices and the possibility of tapped telephones have gradually eroded the illusion that a man's home is his castle. Compared with Luther, however, we spend our days in veritable monastic seclusion. Verbatim records kept by the ubiquitous students made his life an open book.

The blurb on the cover of a modern biography boasts that the author paid two visits a week or so to the home of his subject and so assured the veracity of the writing. The students at Luther's table, scribbling busily day in and day out, have provided us with a mass of firsthand material seldom available to the biographer. The reformer's open life makes it possible for us to see the man in success and failure, strength and weakness, composure and petulance, a saint and a sinner; and the knowledge of it all makes us feel more at home with him.

III

For Luther the choice of a marriage partner was no individual matter. He felt that the family was entitled to make its voice heard in the selection of his mate. While parents had no right to force their children into an objectionable union, children should not become infatuated and make a foolish match. Jacob failed in Luther's eyes because he became enamored of Rachel's pretty face. Luther's ideal was Rebekah, who accepted the mate chosen by her family.

It followed that the reformer saw the dangers of fanciful and unreal ideas about marriage. There were pitfalls in a liason of physical attraction. "Merely sleeping together will not do it alone; there must be unity and harmony of mind, heart, habits and life. Each must be patient and helpful with the other for things cannot always go smoothly."

A recent writer spoke about loving a person from "the head down." He met a girl in a library where she sat behind a desk. As he periodically talked with her, he discovered they had much in common. Then once he met her on the street and inwardly said, "Wowie, you mean that figure goes with the head that I have grown to love." Love from the top of the head down was his advice as it had been Luther's so many years before when he insisted that marriage be based on the sharing of mutual interests.

The grim necessities of eating and living were constantly before Luther, and he urged recognition of the importance for the bride to be trained in the common art of housekeeping. "You would gladly have a beautiful, good, and rich wife if you could. Indeed we really ought to paint you one with red cheeks and white legs! These are the best, but they usually cook poorly and pray badly." [6] His Katie, whose looks had failed to attract a husband, capably presided over his home, efficiently managed their establishment, and thus brought him happiness.

He saw the necessity of a maturing love which continued to develop through marriage. "The first love is drunken. When intoxication wears off, then comes the real marriage love." Husbands and wives must realize the importance of continuing to please each other. Wives were exhorted, "Make your husband glad to come across his threshold at night"; and husbands, "Make your wife sorry when you leave." "Union of the flesh does nothing. There must also be union of manners and mind." The much discussed togetherness of this age can have no better objective than that stated by Luther.

The union didn't always proceed harmoniously. The word-by-word record of Luther's own life, kept by wide-eyed and open-eared students, recounts some of the irritations of married life.

On one occasion while Luther was answering a student's question, Katie interrupted, "Doctor, why don't you stop talking and eat?"

The exasperated reformer-husband replied, "I wish that women would repeat the Lord's Prayer before opening their mouths."

Though often in deadly earnest in his utterances, Luther's sense of humor periodically crept out. The recorded conversation shows him in action.

LUTHER: We shall yet see the day when a man will take several wives.
KATIE: The devil thinks so.
LUTHER: The reason, dear Katie, is that a woman can have only one child a year, whereas a man can beget several.
KATIE: Paul says, "Let each man have his own wife."
LUTHER: Aye, his own wife, but not only one; that is not in Paul.

Thus the doctor joked a long time until Katie said: "Before I would stand for that I would go back to the convent and leave you and all your children!" [7]

Luther who would fight to the death for the principle of monogamy enjoyed teasing his wife about the alleged masculine bent towards polygamy.

Luther did not believe in the modern fifty-fifty marriage. For him the husband was the head of the wife, who was obliged to give him love and honor, but it was the husband's responsibility to rule in love and gentleness.

Such was his theorizing. In practice it was not quite the same. Shortly after their marriage his wife dissuaded him from attending Spalatin's wedding. In the domestic sphere particularly she subtly guided him into the policies *she* thought were best. Luther frequently teased his wife and referred to her as

Master Kate. As the proverb has it, there is many a true word spoken in jest.

The man who had stood up to the might of the medieval church and defied the powerful rulers of his day was no match for the astute ex-nun who influenced him in so many ways.

IV

Luther lived in a day that had not heard of John Dewey or Sigmund Freud or even Rousseau. The permissive philosophies of child-rearing which have called forth the derisive comment that a modern parent never hits a child except in self-defense were foreign to the reformer.

Childhood held few happy memories for Luther. He later recalled, "My mother caned me for stealing a nut, until the blood came." "My father whipped me so that I ran away." Yet Luther had a deep sense of responsibility to his father, and Erickson in his psychological interpretation *The Young Man Luther* has seen in Luther's major life's decisions the working out of relationships with his father.

Entering the monastery had been against his father's wishes. His father relented enough, however, to bring the family to hear Martin say his first mass, and Martin had the date set to suit the older Luther. The great moment proved to be traumatic; as the young monk stood before the altar reciting the words, "We offer unto the true and living God," he was temporarily overcome by a sense of unworthiness and experienced a violent tremor.

At the festive meal that followed, Martin, fresh from the overpowering experience with his Heavenly Father in the saying of the mass, sought reassurance from his earthly parent. He asked his father if he had not changed his mind and overcome the previous disappointment that his son had become a monk. Hans Luther swelled with indignation and berated his son before the assembled company of doctors, masters, and guests. "You learned scholar, have you never read in the Bible that you should honor your father and mother? And here you have left me and your dear mother to look after ourselves in our old age."

When the time came for Luther's marriage, one of the reasons he gave for it was that it would please his father. Martin's prized first-born son was given the name of Hans to honor the older Luther. Paternal loyalty was always strong in Luther's life, yet it was a fidelity reinforced by an agonizing fear.

The reformer came to see the family as a different institution from that in which he himself had grown. It was for him, in Bainton's words, "the school for character." In his own family responsibilities he became increasingly aware of parents' problems—the daily concern for earning the living, difficulties in pregnancy, and trials of rearing children. In exasperation he exclaimed, "Child, what have you done that I should love you so? You have disturbed the whole household with your bawling." When a crying child kept him awake at night he sighed, "This is the sort of thing that caused the church fathers to vilify marriage."

But let there be no misunderstanding; Luther enjoyed family life. His letters to his children are gems of understanding, encouragement, and concern. In one of the most moving of these, he tells of a wonderful garden for good children, "with rosy apples, pears, cherries and fine ponies with golden bridles and silver saddles." [8] He wrote some of the loveliest hymns for children.

Following the labors of the day, the family often gathered together. Luther told them stories, played his lute, taught them songs and games. He composed his Smaller Catechism for children and set the example of leading family worship as the head of the house. On his trips he always tried to remember to bring something for the children, and the ever thoughtful Katie kept a secret store of trinkets in case her absentminded husband forgot.

There were heart-wrenching moments. The death of Magdalena at the tender age of fourteen tore him to pieces. His agonizing prayer was, 'O God, I love her so, but Thy will be done."

To the girl, his words were, "Magdalenchen, my little girl, you would like to stay with your father here and you would be glad to go to your Father in heaven?"

Magdalena replied, "Yes, dear father, as God wills."

The grief-stricken father held the little girl in his arms, and she passed away. For him was the pain as well as the pleasures of family life.

V

Abraham Lincoln is credited with having said that God must have loved ordinary people because He made so many of them. The genius of Luther lay in his link with the common man. His earthy, sometimes crude and coarse language was a sign of his strength as well as his weakness. Taking pen in hand to translate Erasmus' Greek Testament into German, he gave solidity to the tongue of his day. Of this work the scholar Jacob Grimm has said, "Luther's German became the core of the new German language."

Another authority claims Luther's translation of the Lord's Prayer was so striking that "most Germans came to feel that Christ conceived it in German." [9] The infinite God spoke to common man in plain everyday speech.

In his revolt against the medieval church, Luther gave the

world a new concept of the calling of God. Before that time the word *vocation* had had a very limited meaning, being used to describe men and women who felt the call of God to a higher life and had left everyday affairs to retire to monastic seclusion. In this sheltered sanctuary they sought to prepare themselves for heaven. The medieval world consisted of soldiers, saints, and sinners, with the saints safely protected by the monastery wall.

Luther developed a different view of life. He came to see that human work was not a penalty for sin but a response to God's call. The concept of a man's work as a calling has led to the now commonly accepted idea of a vocation. As Luther said it, "There is no special religious vocation since the call of God comes to each man at the common tasks." "The lowlier the task the better. The milkmaid and the carter of manure are doing a work more pleasing to God than the psalm singing of a Carthusian."

It gradually became obvious to the reformer that the sanctity of marriage and family life were logical outcomes of his teaching of the priesthood of all believers. Lazareth notes the evolution of Luther's thought. Up until 1523 he saw marriage as a "remedy against sin." His thought gradually extended until he "extolled marriage as the Christian's highest social calling." [10]

Most of Luther's view of love and marriage makes sense. Marriage was a partnership which, like the rest of life, had been planned by and ordained of God. Parents were to assist the immature young person in making a sensible choice. Many of the modern plans of computerized marriages which decide whether or not the couple are really suited for each other may really represent a swing back to the recognition that much more attention must be paid to the mental and temperamental suitability of the couple for each other.

The much publicized and widely discussed family life of Luther, which was lived "in the goldfish bowl," obviously fulfilled a useful purpose. Bainton claims Luther's home and example did more than any other single factor to determine the tone of German domestic relations for the next four centuries.

From Luther's experience too came a new institution, the Protestant parsonage. Although titles of books such as *That Darn Preacher's Kids* have helped foster the illusion that children of the parsonage are the terror of the neighborhood, the facts are far otherwise. From Protestant parsonages has come a stream of outstanding and influential men and women who have made a unique contribution to our society.

Poor Martin Luther! What strange evaluations men have made of him. Erickson, in his psychiatric evaluation, selects some representatives. Dr. Otto Scheel, a *professor*, with open admiration portrays Luther as the man of God. Heinrich Denifle, a Dominican *priest*, and the greatest critic and detractor of them all, exposes Luther as the depraved psychopath. Dr. Paul J. Reiter, a *psychiatrist*, weighs the evidence to conclude that Luther in his middle forties fell victim to a psychotic episode. A *psychoanalyst*, Professor Preserved Smith considers the reformer "a thoroughly typical example of the neurotic quasi-hysterical sequence of a sex complex." R. Pascal, a *Marxist historian*, regards him as a product of the class struggle propelled by the forces of history.

As varied as his personality undoubtedly was, Luther could hardly have been all of these. Apparently each researcher discovered that for which he sought.

To all these illustrious evaluators might be added a twentieth-century newcomer, the psychologist marriage counselor. This man specializes in helping people through crisis experiences.

Stormy and tempestuous by nature, Luther's life certainly was crisis upon crisis—his being driven to his knees by a thunderclap and vowing to enter a monastery; the bringing on of Erikson's "identity crisis" by the fit in the choir; his springing to his feet at the top of Pilate's stairs to inquire, "Who knows whether this is so?"; his taking of hammer in hand to nail the celebrated ninety-five theses on the door of the Castle Church; his standing before the Diet of Worms, refusing to retract, "Here I stand, I cannot do otherwise."

For the counselor the crisis which may have brought the greatest test of all to Luther is summarized in the words, "The report is true that I suddenly married Katherine." Of all human crises few are more commonly experienced nor more inadequately handled than marriage. This one crisis sets up a chain reaction of crises: the birth of children, financial stress, the launching of children into adult life, and the empty nest.

And in this crisis Luther came through with flying colors, leaving an indelible imprint on our ideas of love, marriage, and family life.

3

Lover on Horseback

John Wesley (1703–1791)

"If we are to have two kings, we must have two beds."

The little man had sprung to his feet, his five feet five and a half inches a tower of indignation. From his vantage point he looked down to deliver the edict to his kneeling spouse.

Unexpectedly caught in the very act, the surprised woman remained frozen in her devotional posture, except for a half-raised head and a startled expression which, like the scudding clouds before the full moon, flitted across her sensitive countenance.

The whole ridiculous tableau symbolized masculine-feminine relationships in the eighteeenth century. As lord of the house, the mighty male, small in stature but tall in status, gazed down from his superior station upon his spouse, who, no matter what order her intelligence or abilities, was his inferior. British law declared the fact, and social practice confirmed it.

Or was she?

In so many ways the obedient wife, Susannah Wesley worked diligently at all her domestic responsibilities and struggled with a half-furnished house, an inadequate income, and dutifully bore a child each year.

Yet Samuel, the rector of Epworth, had a suspicion that under that seemingly yielding obedient femininity there lurked a potential revolutionist striking out against the hallowed status of man. Susannah didn't hesitate to challenge masculine opinions, and every now and then let it be known she was going to have her own ideas, no matter what might be masculine thought.

It seemed to him that the thin veneer of eighteenth-century feminine submissiveness had temporarily peeled during their discussions of fealty to the king. They both agreed on the necessity of loyalty, but to whom?

Samuel gave his undivided allegiance to King William. Susannah saw him just as the "Prince of Orange." The true British king must be a descendant of King James.

So it happened that as they knelt at prayer, the fiery rector had watched his spouse with a suspicious eye. Instead of the "amen" with which she should have dutifully responded after his prayer for His Majesty King William, she mutely knelt with tightly closed lips.

Convinced now of her obstinate spirit, the rector had jumped to his feet to throw down his edict and remained posed like some stone statue.

The sound of a crying child broke the spell; and Samuel dropped his oratorical gesture, pivoted around and stamped out of the room to quickly gather his possessions before heading out for London.

The one certain event in the Wesley household did not eventuate that year. Susannah failed to deliver a baby. It was the only year she missed in all her married years of fertility.

If only for this reason, the birth of that little boy John after a two-year interval might have made him something special. He symbolized reconciliation after one of the most difficult periods in the married life of Samuel and Susannah.

If confirmation of John's uniqueness were needed, it came with the fire. The burning of the Epworth parsonage had an air of intrigue about it. Mysterious events had transpired around the house. The fire that destroyed nearly all the rector's worldly goods may have been started by some disgruntled parishioner; a strained relationship existed between this shepherd and certain members of his flock.

As a dramatic spectacle the fire reached its climactic moment when the head and shoulders of a small six-year-old boy appeared at an upper window. The rest of the family were safely outside, but this little fellow was trapped.

After a valiant but futile effort to reenter the house, the vicar retreated before a wall of flame. In an agony of frustration he threw himself on his knees and committed the soul of his child to God.

More practical-minded men outside the house searched in vain for a ladder, then quickly ran to the wall. While one stood with his back to the quivering structure, a comrade climbed on his shoulders and managed to reach the small boy, yanking him from his precarious perch. The deed was done in the nick of time. The burning roof collapsed with a resounding crash, covering the bystanders with sparks and tinders. By a hair's breadth the small boy had been saved from a horrible death.

As the men carried the boy from the burning building, Mrs. Wesley rushed over to snatch him from the rescuer's arms and

hold him close to her flushed face. To her there was something symbolic about the whole episode. This boy John was
indeed her "brand from the burning."

The incident served to foster an impression Susannah had
long felt. Nearly two years later when John was almost eight
years old, Susannah, in her own exquisite handwriting, wrote
in her meditations, "I do intend to be more particularly careful of the soul of this child that thou hast so mercifully
provided for, than I have been, that I may endeavor to instill
into his mind the principles of true religion and virtue. Lord
give me grace to do it sincerely and prudently; and bless my
attempts with good success."

Susannah worked diligently at her task. She developed an
intensely personal system which she described in a letter to
her husband, "on Monday, I talk with Molly; on Tuesday,
with Hetty; Wednesday, with Nancy; Thursday, with Jackie;
Friday, with Patty; Saturday, with John; and Emily and Sukey
together on Sunday." So she launched her historic teaching
ministry.

Susannah was the first woman to influence John Wesley.
He was her "brand from the burning." She never let him
forget it. In his memory there long lived those Thursday
evenings when he sat and listened as his mother spoke in such
solemn tones.

I

In what John called "dear delightful Stanton" lived the
scintillating Kirkham family. Of the three girls in the family,
Sally stood out as the most attractive. In her younger days her
high spirits had caused Mary Granville's father, who lived
nearby and had heady plans for his daughter, to wonder if

Mary should really be friendly with such a tomboy as Sally. He considered her too much of a fun lover, who did not display the gentle feminine graces and the serious manner thought to be the hallmark of a lady in the eighteenth century.

John, now a student at Oxford University, still a callow youth in terms of social development if not in age, and somewhat shy and aloof, was introduced to the Kirkham family by his friend John Griffith; he responded warmly to the spirit of this lively and affluent group.

As an eligible bachelor, he found himself in the center of an adoring circle of women and enjoying every moment of it. Above all the others stood one lovely, laughing, fascinating girl, Sally Kirkham.

In his diary he wrote, ". . . first saw Varanese (Sally). May it not be in vain." John struggled with his thoughts of Sally. Could anything ever come of this? Did he have any right to ask her to accept the attentions of a poor scholar?

Fifteen years later when John wrote out all the details of his tortuous religious pilgrimage, he was careful to give credit to Sally, whom he referred to as a "religious friend." Although a fun-loving girl, much of her hilarity was a façade for an underlying serious spirit. She delighted to sit in earnest discussion about the deeper things of the religious life.

Having carefully listened to the serious John tell his story of the agony of his spiritual quest, Sally turned spiritual physician. As she saw it, a condition like his called for strong medicine. She prescribed the reading and study of a series of devotional classics, Thomas à Kempis' *Imitation of Christ*, Bishop Jeremy Taylor's *Holy Living and Holy Dying*, William Law's *Christian Perfection*.

"Write it down, Jack." As clearly as if Susannah had been alongside him, John heard her words. As carefully as a merchant kept his accounts so that he could at any time establish his financial situation, John took quill in hand to catalog his spiritual assets and liabilities.

Each time he struck a balance, he apprehensively wondered if he were not on the verge of spiritual bankruptcy. A more impartial auditor might have wondered if the books had not been unwittingly juggled to make the liabilities appear more obvious than the assets.

Long discussions with Sally and the reading of the devotional classics plus the gentle push of his mother led him to apply for ordination. Kneeling on the cold stone floor of Christ Church Cathedral, he became increasingly conscious of the shapely hands of Dr. Porter, the Bishop of Oxford, framed in the white linen cuffs of his surplice.

Gently those fine fingers rested on the head of the earnest young man. As if it were the first blown snow of the winter or perhaps even the heavenly dove, the paraclete, descending from heaven, John became aware of the words. "Take thou the authority to execute the Office of Deacon in the Church of God committed unto thee. In the name of the Father and of the Son and of the Holy Ghost. Amen."

John often pondered the possibility of proposing marriage to Sally. In an academic way he discussed the subject of matrimony with Robin Griffith but inevitably saw his situation as such that he couldn't really marry. He had nothing to offer a wife. Moreover, for some time he had nursed a conviction that for a priest celibacy was the most desirable state.

And then there were finances. The poor Oxford student could hardly manage to keep himself, let alone a wife.

The whole marriage question resolved itself without his help. Sally had already been promised in marriage to the local schoolmaster, John Chapone. Sally gently told John the date had been set for the marriage. He swallowed over and stammered out his congratulations.

John rode silently back to Oxford on the afternoon of the wedding to spend a quiet evening in his lonely room. Turning to his diary he wrote with trembling hand, "May God give her the happiness she deserves."

Of all the strange relationships none was more complex than that of the young priest more than half committed to celibacy and the blissfully happy Mrs. Chapone. After nearly a year of married life, Sally wrote to tell John that her complacent husband had no real objection to their friendship.

Saturday nights were times of testing for John. He had early adopted the practice of spending these evenings in self-examination. The weekly confessional had a burning theme following a trip to Stanton, "Have I loved women or company more than God?"

He stretched out the intervals between his visits to the villages, but like the moth drawn to the flame, he always gravitated back.

In the midst of all the feminine adulation of eligible girls, a married woman, Sally, held John in love devoid of passion. In the course of one long tender conversation, she let him know how much his friendship meant to her. In her eighteenth-century manner she said, "In the number of my friends there is no one, I see, and always shall, in a stronger view than you."

This was the calm before the storm. Two events rocked John's world.

The following day brought the news of Robin Griffith's death. John and Robin had been close friends, and after visiting the bereaved family, who requested him to conduct the funeral service, John gave himself to the task of preparing a funeral sermon.

While working on this melancholy project, Sally's sister Damaris came by to call on him. She broke the news ever so gently. She believed John Chapone was jealous of John Wesley. John was crushed. There was no real reason for jealousy. Or was there? He rode silently back to Oxford that day smarting under two losses, a man and a woman.

II

The correspondence with Sally continued intermittently across the years but it could never be the same again. Perhaps Mary Pendarves had something to do with it.

Mrs. Pendarves had come to call at the Stanton rectory. She received a warm welcome, and Sarah Kirkham embraced her with squeals of delight in a happy reunion of childhood friends.

The attractive young widow had packed many years of living into her short life. Born Mary Granville, she was reared with the idea of a career in the royal court. While on one of her periodic visits to titled relatives during which she stayed with her uncle, Lord Lansdowne, another visitor came to the house, Mr. Pendarves of Cornwall, sixty years old, overweight, awkward, suffering with the gout, and addicted to the bottle. His negligently worn clothes bore the stains of the snuff he so frequently sniffed. Altogether he was less than attractive.

The elderly man had eyes only for the pretty seventeen-year-old. At the earliest convenient moment he contacted her parents suggesting marriage. The idea of marrying someone forty years her senior repelled Mary, but the family gently reminded her that she was getting on in years. Her father had died; the court position had not opened up; and it was rumored that the crusty old man had money.

Six years of married life must have taught her something.

There was little happiness in it. Mary had nicknamed her husband Gromio. His drinking habits grew worse, and the frightened wife hardly knew whether she feared most his raucous inebriation or his gloomy sullen sobriety. In a symbolic climax Mary awakened one morning to find her husband dead in bed at her side.

Mrs. Pendarves was something less than prostrate with grief. The legacy itself proved to be disappointing, but she consoled herself that it was at last her own. At last she had the freedom for which she had longed over the years.

Trying hard to play the role of a distraught widow, Mrs. Pendarves again took up residence with her uncle and aunt, Sir John and Lady Stanley. Here she came in contact with the dashing young Lord Baltimore. A surreptitious romance ripened rapidly. It seemed to be only a matter of waiting for a decent mourning period. Then it all fell through; the lord married another girl.

Mary left for the country to stay with her mother and to see if the balm of the English countryside could bring healing to her wounded spirit.

One Sunday the whole family attended the church at Stanton. The rector was not preaching. An earnest young priest from Oxford occupied the pulpit. As John Wesley preached that morning no one listened more intently than the pretty little widow sitting in the Granville pew.

Following the church service the "in" group adjourned to the rectory where they sat around to drink tea. Mary became the center of all attention as she related the latest news from London and gently hinted at the scandals of the court. A few catty women noticed she did not mention the Baltimore wedding.

John came later to join the group. Sally hastened to receive him and led him straight over to meet Mrs. Pendarves. The young minister politely went through the formalities. The self-possessed young widow overawed John, but manifested an obvious interest, flattering the preacher within him by requesting a copy of his sermon.

The friendship grew. She teasingly called him "Primitive Christianity." While away on a temporary visit to London, she sent a message to her sister, "I honor Primitive Christianity, and desire you will let him know as much when you see him."

Sally rejoiced that John and Mary found each other's company so agreeable. The three of them became inseparable. The vivacious Mary suggested they follow the current court fad and take pseudonyms. Sally was to be Varanese; John, Cyrus; and Mary, Aspasia.

With strange old world courtesy they began the practice of writing three-way letters. Sally entered the enterprise with relish; but it gradually began to dawn on her that although the letters mentioned Varanese, Cyrus and Aspasia, it was really a correspondence between Cyrus and Aspasia.

That all the discussion was not religious is indicated by a hurried postscript Mary added to one of her letters, "I must insist on your burning all my letters, and pray don't use any epithet before my name when you write to me. I have no time to tell my reasons."

John had often warned Mary about the wordly round of social life and the dangers of the lust of the eye and the pride of life. He must have been aware that they offered a particular temptation to this pretty little widow. The pull was too great for John to really oppose it. Social responsibilities beckoned. John heard that Mrs. Pendarves had departed to visit Ireland.

Although she left her address and instructions with her sister for forwarding John's correspondence, he received no reply to his letters. Mary welcomed his solemn epistles, determined to answer them, but never got around to it.

Three years after her departure John received a letter from Mary. She expressed her regret for her lapse in correspondence and said she would happily accept his reproach if she could renew his friendship.

In his answer Wesley showed that he had carefully evaluated the fanciful friendship. With a sigh he wrote, ". . . for some time I flattered myself with the pleasing hope; but I grew more and more ashamed of having indulged it. You need not the support of so weak a hand."

It had ended. A happy memory which would soon be pushed into the background of a busy life.

Their lives ran in two different directions. Mary had moments when she felt the tug of commitment to the way of the sober and methodical John, but the social world silenced the still small voice.

Nothing could stop her. After the disappointing experiences of earlier days, Mary married Dr. Delany, the Dean of Down. Her list of friends reads like a "Who's Who" of eighteenth-century England. It includes Dean Swift, Samuel Johnson and King George III. Edmund Burke said of her that she was "the highest bred woman in the world."

The austere John continued his work toward saving his soul. His pathway led him across the Atlantic to far-off America where he lived under a set of circumstances as different as could be imagined from the round of receptions, balls, and operas that occupied the days of Mrs. Delany, formerly Mrs. Pendarves, née Mary Granville, alias Aspasia.

III

Sophia needed help. She lived with her uncle and aunt, Mr. and Mrs. Thomas Causton. Although Mr. Causton held the important position of magistrate of the colony, his somewhat dubious record in public affairs left him with a number of skeletons in his closet. Some time after his encounter with Wesley, he was expelled from Georgia with a charge of carelessness in money matters hanging over his head.

A chirpy little woman, Mrs. Causton's bird brain flitted easily from one subject to another, alighting for a few brief moments before taking off after some more attractive morsel of gossip. Conscious of Sophia's inheritance, she had hastened to clasp her to her ample bosom. Enthusiasm soon waned, and with her husband, she hoped that Sophy would find some eligible suitor to take her off their hands.

Sophia's love life was just as unfortunate as her family circumstances. Tom Mellicamp had wooed her. A turbulent young man, he had a tempestuous and passionate nature. In one stormy scene, Tom threatened Sophia, telling her that if she married someone else it would be a funeral instead of a wedding.

The saintly young Anglican priest John Wesley was quite different from Sophia Hopkey's guardian, boyfriend, or for that matter any other man she had encountered in her brief life.

When John fell ill from eating food about which he had a question, in his guilty agony he looked up into the face of the woman who had come to care for him. For five days she gave him her undivided attention. Although he had met her before at the church services, he now saw her through different eyes. Dressed in white, for she had learned that the young minister disliked showy clothes, she looked to John like an angel of mercy.

This soft, sweet girl who had been so kind to him now needed his help. As she tended him, she related her story of spiritual difficulty. With characteristic concern Wesley volunteered to become both her spiritual director and teacher. She longed for a deeper spiritual life and was particularly inter-

ested in learning French. The handsome young minister prepared himself for the not so onerous task of instructing his
attractive pupil.

John moved from Savannah to Fort Frederica. It seemed as
if he were forever making the miserable and monotonous
one-hundred-mile trip between Savannah and the fort.

The fact that Sophia had preceded him to Frederica helped.
A joyful reunion followed. Sophy resumed her French lesson
under John's tutelage. This added to his work, but it made
Frederica look much better to John's eyes.

When it came time for Wesley to return to Savannah,
Oglethorpe suggested Sophia go along with him. Delighted at
first, John found his joy changing to apprehension. The gover-
nor smiled as he told John that he and Sophy would be the
only passengers on the trip.

Although Savannah was only one hundred miles away it
took the flat-bottomed craft at least six days to make the
journey. With the close of day they would go ashore and pitch
camp for the night. Anything might happen.

Determined to overcome lethargy with action, Wesley led
off on the first day of the trip by reading Bishop Patrick's
prayer. Later in the afternoon he turned to Fleury's *History of
the Church* for Sophy's edification. His pious hope was that
she would appreciate the magnificent example set by the ancient Christians who stood steadfast in their faith.

In the course of that difficult trip, John observed her patient
spirit and capacity to suffer. They engaged in long and serious
discussions on subjects like "Lying in order to do good" and
Christian holiness.

One night they slept on an island beneath the sheltering
canvas. Little tongues of flame flickered spasmodically from
the slowly burning fire. As John lay there, he found great
difficulty in sleeping. He looked toward Sophia, and by the

dancing light saw that she too was awake. They began to talk. He mentioned the impulsive young man who had recently wooed her. She sweetly replied that she had no real interest in Tom and had given no commitment in this relationship.

In this dramatic moment Wesley heard himself saying, "Miss Sophy, I should think myself happy if I were to spend my life with you."

Sophia had been well trained. She made the appropriate eighteenth-century response by bursting into tears. She sobbed out that she was in such a mixed-up state she could not marry anybody. Nevertheless she left the subject open adding that when others spoke to her about marriage she had been repelled. She smiled sweetly as she told him there were no feelings like this in her heart at the moment.

All was set for a declaration. Lapping water, twinkling stars, and the black velvet backdrop of night. The dear, sweet, tear-stained face. The darling girl waiting to be comforted.

But John had had his answer. All this subtlety was beyond him. People meant what they said. The lady had spoken. She did not intend to marry anybody.

John broke the silence, "Let me read a psalm."

Blessed is the man that hath not walked in the counsel of the ungodly, nor stood in the way of sinners, and hath not sat in the seat of the scornful. But his delight is in the law of the Lord; and in his law will he exercise himself day and night.

And he shall be like a tree planted by the water side, that will bring forth his fruit in due season . . .[1]

John's voice tapered away as he settled back to sleep.

The puzzled Sophy had much more difficulty in sleeping.

Settling into parish life in Savannah, this committed bachelor, John, was seized with a sense of foreboding. He confided his inner turbulence to the pages of his personal diary, "I now began to be much afraid. My desire and design was still to live single; but how long it would continue I knew not." But like the bird mesmerized by the snake and moving ever closer, John, despite his awareness of the danger, spent long hours each day with Sophy. He periodically fortified himself with the time-honored method of protection of concluding each visit by reading a psalm.

Then came what he was to refer to as his "narrow escape." One day they sat talking together, and Wesley found himself hinting about marriage. Sophia expressed the opinion that she herself felt it best a clergyman should not marry so that he would not be encumbered with worldly cares. She further stated that she herself had reached the conclusion it would be unwise for her to marry. Wesley adds, "I used no argument to induce her to alter her resolution."

A somewhat surprised Sophia received a letter from John. It read, "I find, Miss Sophy, I can't take fire in my bosom, and not be burnt. I am retiring therefore for a while to desire the direction of God. Join with me, friend, in fervent prayer, that He should show me what is best to be done."

John had retired to Irene but found that it wasn't as easy to get away from Sophy. Physical distance could not stop his active imagination. Absence made the heart grow fonder. He wrestled with "unholy desire." He wrote in his diary, "My heart was with Miss Sophy all the time. I longed to see her, were it but for a moment."

On Saturday, the 26th of February, John had another narrow escape. He called at the Causton home. He and Sophy were alone. Propinquity spelt danger. Sophy looked as lovely as ever. He later recorded his reactions in his diary, "This was indeed an hour of trial. Her words, her eyes, her hair, her every motion and gesture, were full of such softness and sweetness! I know not what might have been the consequence had I then but touched her hand. And how I avoided it I know not. Surely God is over all!"

His bachelor friends watched with apprehension and horror as Wesley flitted in and out of a potential venture into matrimony. Again he sat down and talked over the matter with them. They finally agreed on the necessity of discovering the Divine Will. After a period of discussion, fasting, and prayer, they decided the best way of finding God's will was to cast lots. Upon three pieces of paper were written "Marry," "Think no more of it this year," and "Think of it no more."

When the lot was drawn, it was, "Think of it no more." God had spoken. Wesley now had his mind made up—marriage was not for him.

To help with the weakness now so noticeable in their leader, the Holy Club made another provision. Physical proximity obviously placed him in a position of jeopardy. They drew lots again to determine if Wesley should ever actually talk with Miss Sophy again. The oracle spoke. The paper drawn said, "Only in the presence of Mr. Delamotte." So John was to be spared the temptation of being alone with Miss Sophy.

Despite this decision, Wesley constantly thought of Sophia and tried to see her. After one encounter he recorded his thoughts, "She went, and I saw myself in the toils. But how to escape I saw not. If I continued to converse with her, though not alone, I found I should love her more. And the time to break it off was past. I felt it was now beyond my strength. My resolutions indeed remained. But how long? Yet a little longer, till another shock of temptation, and then I well knew they would break in sunder as a thread of two that has touched the fire. I had many times prayed that if it was best our intercourse should break off, and that if I could not do it she might. But this too I saw less and less reason to expect. So that all these things were against me, and I lay struggling in the net; nay, scarcely struggling, as even fearing to be delivered."

Liberation came from an unexpected quarter. Pressured by her uncle and aunt and having given up all hope that Wesley would ever propose, Sophia became Mrs. Williamson on March 12, 1737.

The remaining months of Wesley's American ministry were overshadowed by his reaction of frustration and turmoil at Sophia's marriage. He denied her communion and finally left America to return to England as he evaded a warrant for his arrest, which came in part from his alleged slander of Mrs. Williamson.

Exactly one year after Sophia's marriage, John sat down to write an account of the whole affair with Sophia in which he portrayed the episode with a new objectivity. As if a concerned Providence wished to reward his honesty, his Aldersgate Street experience followed. He describes it: "In the evening I went very unwillingly to a society in Aldersgate Street, where one was reading Luther's preface to the Epistle to the Romans. About a quarter before nine, while he was describing the change which God works in the heart through faith in Christ, I felt my heart strangely warmed. I felt I did trust in Christ, Christ alone, for my salvation; and the assurance was given me that He had taken away my sins, even mine, and saved me from the law of sin and death."

From this experience he went out on a crusade now referred to by historians as the Wesleyan Revival.

IV

Grace Murray, the wife of Captain Alexander Murray, having buried her baby, fell into deep depression. In this frame of mind, she went to hear Wesley preach. Her inner turmoil prepared her for the message he brought. At Wesley's meeting she was so overcome that she collapsed on the floor and only walked to her home with the aid of two of the society sisters.

One of the sisters, Maria Price, finally helped Grace find her spiritual feet by reading from the fifth chapter of the Epistle to the Romans. As Maria read, Grace came into the same conversion experience as Wesley had in Aldersgate Street.

Her husband objected to her new religious convictions and threatened to have her committed to a "mad house." The conclusion of it all was both good and bad: good in that Alexander was converted; bad because when the ship *Prince Frederick* returned, it brought the news that during the voyage Alexander Murray had been drowned.

Grace proved to be a convert who meant business. She displayed an unusual talent for evangelistic work, and in a short time Wesley was able to move her into positions of leadership. First as a leader of a band, then as a class leader and later housekeeper of the orphan house, ultimately she was selected by John as one of the inner circle of men and women who accompanied him on his journeys across England and Ireland.

This attractive young woman not only suffered with long periods of depression but also gave other evidences of psychological difficulties. She had strange obsessive reactions after her marriage to Alexander Murray. While attending meetings prior to her conversion, she was several times over "struck down and fell to the ground," and lay there groaning for a thirty-minute period. Morbid dreams periodically bothered her. Long sieges of doubt were her constant companion. She did not find it easy to relate to the women with whom she worked.

Grace's special skill lay in nursing. She cared for many of the outstanding Methodist leaders in their bouts of illness.

None needed the help more than the young gentleman named John Bennet. His serious fever meant a twenty-six weeks' stay in the Orphan House with Grace giving him her careful attention. A bond gradually grew between patient and nurse; when he left the house, they had an understanding that they would keep up correspondence with each other.

Wesley took ill. He went to the Orphanage in Newcastle where Grace cared for him. From his sick bed he had a chance to observe her closely. As he watched the long hours she so willingly spent with him, and how patiently she thought of his every need, he began to realize the loneliness of his bachelor life. What a wonderful blessing it would be if he could have a girl like Grace around constantly.

Looking back on it later he could not remember just how he had slid into it, but the words came from his lips, "If ever I should marry, I think you will be the person."

Grace's eyes filled with tears. John went on to explain how they could share life and the things they might jointly accomplish together.

She leaned over and responded in a voice rich with emotion, "This is too great a blessing for me. I can't tell how to believe it. This is all I could have wished for under heaven, if I dared to wish it."

John took Grace with him on his journeys through Yorkshire and Devonshire. When they arrived at John Bennet's home, Wesley decided it would probably be better for Grace not to continue with the party. He knew not what he said when he exhorted Bennet, "Take great care of Mrs. Murray."

The sight of Grace stirred old memories in John Bennet. They spent a long evening in front of the dancing flames of the fire. They felt so comfortable in each other's company. In this warm glow of fellowship, Bennet asked Grace to become his wife. Grace nodded her head in agreement.

Grace Murray, the former servant girl, found herself promised in marriage to one of the most outstanding preachers of Methodism and also the leader of the whole movement.

A surprised Wesley received two letters. John Bennet's missive sought John's permission to marry Mrs. Murray. Grace's letter reported that she felt it was the will of God that she become Mrs. Bennet.

With the recollection of his own recent avowal, Wesley had some questions in his mind but accepted the situation philosophically. He concluded they had already tied the marriage knot. Taking it all with good grace, John wrote affectionate letters to each of them. With an almost fatal resignation he submitted to the inevitable.

Grace dashed off a grateful note of thanks but waved in the winds of the attraction of these two men. She wrote yet another letter telling John she had changed her mind and wanted him. Then a letter from Bennet convinced her he was the one. But when Bennet failed to arrive for a planned meeting, she ran to Wesley.

They spent long hours in conversation. John, as much in love as any smitten adolescent, made a diary entry, "The more we talked together, the more I loved her." He determined to nail down the relationship. They solemnly entered into a contract de praesenti. This had the force of a definite commitment to each other for marriage.

Wesley had always appeared attractive to females. Many women were drawn to him, and one of these female admirers complicated John and Grace's relationship. To Grace's ears came false and malicious gossip about Wesley and one Molly Francis. The story touched a sensitive nerve, and in a fit of jealousy, Grace wrote to John Bennet reminding him of past days together.

The next day saw her overcome with remorse. In contrition she sought out Wesley to tell him of her foolish action.

But it was too late. John Bennet replied to her letter with enthusiasm. He rejoiced at the prospect of renewing their relationship.

Wesley pondered the situation. He felt they should let things remain as they were until they made their next trip north. Then it would be possible for the three of them to have a face-to-face discussion.

A confrontation followed in Epworth in Lancashire. The two Johns sat down together to talk out the whole matter. When Bennet told John that Grace had sent all of Wesley's letters to him, Wesley began to have second thoughts. He left Bennet's house that night conceding Grace to his rival.

The break of day saw Wesley hard at work writing. He worked on a letter to Grace. In it he told her he thought it only right that she should marry Bennet whom she obviously loved more than him. John had had enough of it all. He finished his letter, "I think it best that you and I should not meet each other again. Farewell."

The letter revived Grace's affection for John, and she responded with fervent protestations of her love. John remained in an agony of uncertainty for several days. Finally on Wednesday, September the 6th, he went to Grace. He was careful to record the very words he used, "Which will you chuse?"

Grace hesitated not a moment, "I am determined by conscience as well as by inclination, to live and die with you."

One of the conditions John had laid down to Grace was that before he married, his brother Charles should be consulted. John wrote Charles a letter telling him the news of the impending marriage.

Of all the people he might have consulted, Charles was

undoubtedly the worst. A remarkably gifted man, Charles Wesley wrote the texts of some of the most beautiful religious songs in our hymnals. Nevertheless, he was, to put it mildly, an impulsive individual.

John's letter infuriated him. He began to inquire around about the background of John's romance. In his first consultation with them, Robert Swendell and William Shent told Charles that Grace Murray was really engaged to John Bennet.

Charles jumped onto his horse's back and rode madly off to the place where he believed Grace and John had established their love nest. Somewhat chagrinned, he discovered John alone.

Charles poured out his scorn on the whole matrimonial project. John had no right even to consider marriage. Charles had recently married a woman of noble birth. Self-righteously, he insisted if John were to marry, he must not venture into matrimony with anybody so lowborn as Grace.

He became a prophet of gloom. He predicted dire calamity for their work. If John were to marry Grace chaos would come upon the societies. He painted a tumultuous picture of preachers withdrawing from the groups and societies ingloriously disbanding.

Charles' attack unnerved John, and he immediately sat down to consider all the objections there might be to this marriage. Having written them all down along with the answers, he was finally able to write down, "My seven arguments against marriage are totally set aside. Nay, some of them seem to prove that I ought to marry, and that Grace Murray is the person."

Meanwhile Charles in a meeting with Grace charged that if she married John it would be the ruination of both John and the societies. Convinced she must do the right thing, Grace Murray became Mrs. John Bennet, October 3, 1749.

V

Preparing for a trip north, John slipped. Literally slipped. On the ice, as he crossed a London bridge, and he badly hurt his ankle bone. The surgeon attended him and bound up the damaged limb.

He struggled on to Seven Dials where he preached that morning. After a trying afternoon he proceeded to the Foundry for the evening service. By this time the pain was excruciating, and he found it impossible to preach. John was persuaded to rest for a few days, and he limped off to the home of Mrs. Vazeille on Threadneedle Street where she undertook to care for him.

Wesley remained seven days in the Vazeille home. The days were spent, he tells us, "in prayer, reading, and conversation, and partly writing a Hebrew grammar and Lessons for Children." Later events suggest the conversation was obviously of considerable importance.

A whirlwind courtship followed. Wesley had his accident on Sunday, February the 10th. Eight days later, February the 18th, he and Mrs. Vazeille were joined together in holy matrimony. His ankle was still so painful that he could not stand on his leg for the wedding ceremony.

John and Molly left on a honeymoon occupied with something less than romantic activities. John decided this would be an opportune time for him to visit the London societies. The newlyweds received a warm welcome, and John enjoyed the experience although his damaged leg compelled him to kneel while preaching.

A strained relationship existed between John and Charles. The hurt of the Grace Murray episode was long in healing. John wrote to Charles to tell his brother he had decided to marry, but didn't mention the name of his bride-to-be. When Charles learned it was Mrs. Vazeille, he spent a day in lamentation; but the relationship with John was so deteriorated that nothing could be done.

Molly Vazeille of all people! Coming from a family of meager means, she had taken the only course open for a girl of her station in life and gone into domestic service. While she worked at her menial tasks, she dreamed of living the life that her mistress enjoyed. Then came her opportunity when the widowed Noah Vazeille asked her to be his wife.

The impoverished background and years in service had left her with an urge to dominate. She soon learned that the long-suffering Noah Vazeille would do anything she wanted if she kept after him for long enough. He humored her every whim; and when he died, he left her and the children a small fortune.

When Wesley faced the possibility of marrying girls as outstanding as Sophy and Grace, he vacillated, inquired of friends, thought it over, procrastinated, and finally waited so long that a rival moved in and snatched his love object away from him. Now like the traditional fool, he rushed in where angels feared to tread. He temporarily forgot his own "rules for a helper" which required a preacher to seek the opinion of his friends before marrying.

John had been rethinking his attitude toward marriage. In the searching self-examination which was so much a part of his relationship with Grace Murray, he had faced the whole question of his objections against marriage and answered these one by one. There had come a final settlement in his mind.

John met with the men of the London Society. These single

men broached the subject of marriage. The preacher, at this time forty-eight years of age and unmarried himself, listed the advantages of not being married. He commended celibacy, naming it as a gift to remain single for the sake of the Kingdom of Heaven. While he conceded there might be exceptions to this rule, he made no bones about the advantages of the celibate servant of God. This happened just ten days before his marriage.

Was John trying to prove something? He had been disappointed with Charles after his marriage. Charles' zeal for traveling and preaching had abated. He had noted that preachers who were married gave less time to preaching after losing their single status.

Determined to show that his marriage would not interfere with his Christian calling, just two weeks after his flight into matrimony, John set out on his mission rounds, leaving his new bride behind him. In the course of this journey, he made a notable entry in his journal, "I cannot understand how a Methodist Preacher can answer it to God, to preach one sermon, or travel one day less, in a married than in a single state."

Forty-eight years old at the time of his marriage, Wesley had reached a stage of development in which bachelors used to a single existence are not very good marriage risks. It is highly improbable that an unmarried man of forty-eight will have the flexibility to make the adjustments so important for a successful venture into matrimony.

Wesley had no vision of a home where he could sit by the fire with his children gathered around while he instructed them and gave himself in selfless dedication to rearing his family. He had seen his mother do this. She had invested her life that she might produce missionaries. He was the missionary product and he was determined to fulfill his destiny.

One biographer referred to him as "the happy traveler." His life was an eternal peregrination. The almost incredible distances he traveled in an age when communication was so poor and the means of transportation so bad are almost beyond our comprehensions today.

In his early days he had a conviction that it was best that the preacher should not spend more than six to eight weeks with any one congregation.

Wesley was convinced he should set the example. His commitment to a traveling ministry is seen in the statement which he made to Molly when they were married, "If I thought I should travel one mile less because I was married, as well as I love you, I would never see your face anymore."

Molly believed a woman's place to be in the house. Her domestic efficiency had appealed to John, but husband and wife had different ideas about the chain of command in the Wesley household. Molly saw John through different eyes from those of his followers. He might be the leader of Methodism, but at home he was just a member of the family and as such must come to heel.

Wesley saw it differently. The home in which he lived provided a means of fulfilling his ministry. The demands of a dominant woman who sought to rule the house with a heavy hand became a source of irritation to this itinerant leader.

Wesley's departure from the house provided Molly with a golden opportunity for one of her favorite pastimes. Like a detective hot on the trail of an elusive criminal, she feverishly searched through his room to see what incriminating evidence she could discover. Wesley kept a daily diary, a journal, and also wrote and received many letters. For a wife with a paranoid suspicion about her husband, these letters, diaries, and journals provided a happy hunting ground.

Some of the papers vexed her. She hated Sarah Ryan and

immediately confiscated any letter to or from Sarah. She also had suspicions of the Crosby woman and appropriated her letters. So too, the letters from Mrs. Handley. Nothing incriminating; but one never knew. She kept them just in case.

She checked up on John's finances periodically and felt a housewife's justification in appropriating any surplus money. Like the modern man who objects to having his pockets searched by his wife, Wesley protested these activities. But his writings were his treasures. The carefully kept journal was a priceless possession. When Molly found parts of it that referred to her, or to other women to whom she objected, she adopted the simple expedient of tearing out the offending pages.

The earlier years of Molly's life had been spent at a much lower social level. So long as she kept herself under control, she was very much the model middle-class matron. Dignified and icily correct, she presented a front of respectability to the world. But let one of those ignorant servants make some trivial mistake and all the middle-class veneer would fall away. She would berate the unfortunate servant from her ample supply of invective carefully stored from earlier days.

As the Wesley home grew more irksome, John lost himself in his work, spending long hours laboring in the societies with little time left to be spent at home.

Molly mulled over the matter and decided on a dramatic gesture. She would leave the home of Methodism's leader and advertise to all the world just how impossible it was to live with him.

After having carefully presented a bill of particulars of her complaints to John, Molly gathered all her goods; in January, 1758, she left the Wesley household determined never to return again. As much as John hated it, he braced himself and let her leave.

There were later reconciliations but none of them very effective.

One laconic entry of January, 1771, tells us that he did not dismiss his wife nor would he ask her to come back. He says, "Wednesday 23rd—for what cause I know not . . . set out for Newcastle, purposing 'never to return.' "

In a letter which he wrote to Molly in 1778, Wesley displayed an uncharacteristic bitterness: "If you were to live a thousand years, you could not undo the mischief you have done; and until you have done all you can towards it, I bid you farewell."

VI

A well-known picture shows Wesley in old age. The years dealt gently with him, giving him a position of leadership and respect and setting the lines of his countenance into gentle repose. On the top righthand corner of his picture is a coat of arms inscribed, "God is love."

Wesley's preaching magnified love—the love of God. In his personal counsel his friends noticed his particular interest in young people and their experiences of love. His seven sisters looked upon him as their confidant and bombarded him with a constant stream of letters as they told about their unfortunate love experiences and made him into an eighteenth-century "Dear Abby." He loved his fellow-man and spent himself in self-giving service.

And all of this may have come to pass because of the failure of his love for women. His love affairs were a series of fiascos that inevitably drove him on in his efforts to love both God and his fellow-man.

4

My Dear Dizzy

Benjamin Disraeli (1804–1881)

It is sometimes said the Victorians knew very little about sex but a lot about love. From that period of English history came not only the burgeoning of British colonialism and some of the most idealistic notions of life, but the flowering of romance in the age of naval might, military grandeur, and an empire upon which the sun never set. Presiding over her dominion with strait-laced puritanical ideas, the name of the queen of England identifies this period of history which with all its failures and shortcomings represented one of the most memorable epochs of mankind.

Frequently referred to as the era of "household romanticism," the Victorian period produced stories which, while they appear snobbish and pedantic from our perspective, nevertheless show us some of the most prized human virtues. With studied courtesy, painfully aware of the conventions of a society filled with the new merchants and industrialists anxiously following the customs of aristocracy, the personalities of this age move like shadowy figures on a stage, politely portraying an elegance of manners which called for a self-discipline largely lost in our modern-day society.

Household romanticism is no more clearly seen than in the life of Benjamin Disraeli. Of well-to-do parentage but with the disadvantage of Hebrew ancestry, a foppish manner, and inordinate vanity, this literary upstart of his day became the most picturesque British prime minister of the nineteenth century. And in the shadows lurked Mary Anne.

With an outlandish taste in clothes, tactless in speech, addressing her idol as "Dizzy," she stands beside him as his inspiration and partner. She was able to say, "Dizzy married me for my money; but if he had the chance again, he would marry me for love."

I

The young Disraeli gave little indication of the place he was later to carve for himself in history. Benjamin saw his Jewish father leave the religion of his ancestors and forsake the synagogue, not so much from conviction, but rather in the knowledge that under British law Jews and Catholics were excluded from certain civil rights, and consequently from many of life's opportunities.

The older Disraeli took his children one by one to St. Andrew's Church, where they were duly baptized and made members of the Church of England. For Benjamin this event took place in his thirteenth year. But baptismal waters could not wash away his features, and bigotry would constantly raise its accusing finger to point out his Jewishness.

Youthful years were a combination of intensive study, aimless wandering, fruitless speculation, and growing ambition to make some mark as an author. The possibility of a political career beckoned and with it the idea of making a greater impression on the London of his day.

With this in mind, he decided on a prolonged Mediterranean tour. His future brother-in-law, Meredith, accompanied him as traveling companion and planned to marry Disraeli's favorite sister, Sarah, when he returned. The Mediterranean world captivated Disraeli, and his extravagant dress pulled the eyes of that society upon him. If attention were all he craved, he triumphed.

Unfortunately, while he was in Egypt, Sarah's bridegroom-to-be contracted smallpox and died. Sarah's grief overshadowed the return to the ancestral home, but through her tears she assured her brother she would never marry and that she intended to devote her life to him.

This act of feminine commitment may have set the tone for Disraeli's future and given him a hint as to the direction of his peculiar power. He would enter politics through the salons of London society women. His outlandish dress attracted attention as he appeared in a coat of velvet, open enough in front to reveal a scarlet waistcoat from which extended rather long thin legs covered with poppy-colored trousers braided with gold. Over his white kid gloves rings sparkled and reflected the light.

Staid British males might look upon him with contempt, but his flamboyant garb plus his charming manner won over the feminine hearts.

To his ever growing list of failures in the practical sphere,

Disraeli added a series of business disasters; gradually but inevitably he dissipated the family fortune. Thoughts of marriage crossed his mind—for money maybe, but certainly not for love. He had his friends in stitches of laughter as he said, "As for 'love,' all my friends who have been married for love and beauty either beat their wives or live apart from them. This is literally the case. I may commit many follies in life, but I never intend to marry for 'love' which I am sure is a guarantee of infelicity."

The women flattered him with their attention. He wrote of one to his sister Sarah. "I was introduced 'by particular desire,' to Mrs. Wyndham Lewis, a pretty little woman, a flirt, and a rattle; indeed, gifted with a volubility I should think unequalled, and of which I can convey no idea. She told me that she liked 'silent, melancholy men.' I answered 'that I had no doubt of it.' "

Mrs. Wyndham Lewis chanced to be the wife of a member of parliament, a fact of greatest significance in Disraeli's future.

In his first contest for a seat in parliament, he was defeated, and again in his second. Disappointment flooded over him. He had discovered his oratorical powers. Visiting the House of Commons he disdainfully noted the poor quality of the speeches, "I could floor them all. . . . the time will come." In his private diary he wrote, "I could rule the House of Commons although there would be a great prejudice against me at first."

Disraeli continued as the idol of the women. He had a mistress, already married to another, but responsive and expensive, eating up his meager resources in her demands for parties and suppers. His supreme love, however, continued to be for that fickle mistress called power.

Through feminine acquaintances he made contacts with

men in political office. On one evening, by the grace of Caroline Norton, he met Lord Melbourne, a regular visitor to her home. The loquacious Disraeli attracted the older man, who, in an indulgent moment, asked, "What do you want to be?"

"I want to be prime minister."

The experienced politician smiled indulgently, "Put these foolish ideas out of your head."

So much for Benjamin's dreams.

The death of William IV brought the eighteen-year-old Victoria to the throne and with it new elections. Disraeli received an invitation from Wyndham Lewis to share with him in running for two seats in the safe constituency of Maidstone. Mrs. Wyndham Lewis had thought of him. Disraeli had once referred to her as "that insufferable woman," but as he came to know her, he grew to be more appreciative.

While he increasingly enjoyed her presence and encouragement, she for her part predicted greatness in the years ahead and referred to him as her parliamentary protégé. The election results saw him in a new status, Benjamin Disraeli, M.P. (member of Parliament), and this in no small measure because of the interest of a talkative little woman.

At last, the moment of his dreams: after studied self-discipline in keeping his seat in the historic House of Commons, he was on his feet to deliver his maiden speech. Disaster. No hushed silence nor tumultuous cheer. Laughter, interjection, jeering, ridicule. In agony the speech concluded with a half-defiant statement to the speaker of the House, "Aye, sir, and though I sit down now, the time will come when you will hear me."

Gradually he set about rebuilding his image. The next time he spoke there was no flourish nor strained rhetoric, but just a simple statement of fact—and in a field in which he was thoroughly conversant. Perhaps the memory of the former ungenerous reception struck them, but the members of the house were courteous and attentive. Writing to his sister Sarah, the politician made his prophecy, "Next time I rise in the house, I shall sit down amidst loud cheers."

Six months after taking his seat in the House of Commons came news of the death of his colleague Wyndham Lewis. Disraeli had become increasingly close to these friends of recent days. The closing in of creditors had limited his social life, causing him to spend increasingly more time in the Lewis' home. And now his friend was gone.

He tried to comfort the widow. In one letter he reminded her of the constancy of his friendship and offered to make any contribution to her "welfare or solace" that he could. The regularity of the visits began to extend beyond the concern for a colleague's widow. With the coronation of Queen Victoria came a commemorative gold medal. Such prizes were normally immediately passed on to his ever devoted sister Sarah, but Disraeli gave this particular one to Mrs. Wyndham Lewis.

II

Disraeli's first impressions of Mary Anne Wyndham Lewis were anything but good. When his hostess at a social function asked him to escort her in to dinner, he replied, "Anything rather than that insufferable woman"; finally he muttered, "However, . . . great is Allah," and resigned himself to his fate.

Their ages differed; she was forty-five, he had attained his thirty-third birthday. While she had an income, it could never become his; the terms of her legacy meant it ceased with her death.

In a snobbish Victorian society she often showed an appalling ignorance. She never could remember whether the Greeks or the Romans came first, she was talkative and tactless, and she had a freakish taste in furniture and clothing.

The brilliant Disraeli had seen many outstanding women. He had moved among the high society of London and listened to their dilettante conversation. He was not seeking a competitor. He wanted understanding, flattery, and companionship. In his frequent moments of uncertainty and self-doubt, he needed someone to whom he could turn, and Mary Anne obviously held him in such high esteem. So there came his declaration of love as he proposed that Mary Anne should share life with him.

Of course, the talkative little woman felt flattered; but she who had previously been so flirtatious and anxious to hang on his every word, now realized it is one thing to look longingly at a love object impossible of attainment and yet another to share life with a colorful romanticist. As a friend whose career she fostered he was charming and attractive, but what sort of husband would he make? In the quaint Victorian fashion of that day, she asked for a year in which to contemplate and evaluate before making her decision.

Ever the romantic, Disraeli suffered the agonies of uncertain love. He gave himself to writing and sent a daily epistle to Mary Anne to keep her abreast of his activities. The member of Parliament waxed warm in his writing, "I envy the gentlemen about you, but I am not jealous. When the eagle leaves you, the vultures return." Later, "I feel I can conquer the world." With passing days ardor mounted: ". . . I wish to be with you, to live with you, never be away from you—I care not where in heaven or in earth, or the waters under the earth."

Second thoughts came to the lady. Her letters tapered off. A painful meeting eventuated. Mary Anne had been warned by friends about this adventurer who was willing to change political parties so easily that he must be lacking in loyalty. Heavily in debt, rumor had it that he wanted to marry an older woman with money and thus fend off the money lenders and gain a home in which to live. These and other facts became clear in the course of the interview of Disraeli with the woman he loved.

Disraeli came away fighting mad. The tongue and pen were his weapons. For once his pervasive arguing had failed, and he determined to settle it all with one final edict. He took pen in hand to write a scorching letter, and in a notable flight of rhetoric dismissed his beloved to an awful future: "There will be a final hour of retribution; then you will think of me with remorse, admiration and despair: then you will recall to your memory the passionate heart that you have forfeited, and the genius you have betrayed."

It proved to be a master stroke. Almost in panic Mary Anne replied, "For God's sake come to me. . . . I am devoted to you." She made a notable entry in her account book, "Married 28-8-39. Dear Dizzy became my husband."

III

Mary Anne provided just what Disraeli needed. Very much aware of her responsibilities to him, and in what seems like an exercise that might be expected in a modern psychologically orientated American, she sat down and drew up a series of statements which seemed to her to reflect their personalities.

Him	*Her*
Very calm.	Very effervescent.
Manners grave and almost sad.	Gay and happy-looking when speaking.
Never irritable.	Very irritable.
Bad-humoured.	Good-humoured.
Warm in love, but cold in friendship.	Cold in love, but warm in friendship.

Very patient.	No patience.
Very studious.	Very idle.
Often says what he does not think.	Never says anything she does not think.
It is impossible to find out whom he likes or dislikes from his manner.	Her manner is quite different, and to those she likes she shows her feelings.
No vanity.	Much vanity.
Conceited.	No conceit.
No self-love.	Much self-love.
He is seldom amused.	Everything amuses her.
He is a genius.	She is a dunce.
He is to be depended on to a certain degree.	She is not to be depended on.
His whole soul is devoted to politics and ambition.	She has no ambition and hates politics.

Mary Anne acknowledged she was "a dunce" and "very effervescent," and the combination gave rise to some embarrassing situations. Moving in the high society of the nobility of England, she was constantly putting her foot in her mouth. As some ladies discussed the beauty of Greek statues, she said, "Oh, but you ought to see my Dizzy in his bath!" When staying in the home of a sedate woman, she addressed her hostess, "Oh, I find your house is packed with improper pictures. There's a horrible one in our room. Dizzy says it is Venus and Adonis. I had to stay awake half the night to keep him from looking at it."

One morning, after the pair had spent the night in the room next to that of Lord Hardinge, she said to the latter at breakfast: "Oh, Lord Hardinge, I think I must be the happiest of women! When I woke up this morning, I said to myself: 'How lucky I am! I've been sleeping between the greatest orator and the greatest soldier of the day!' "

Some might laugh, but not Disraeli.

On one occasion one of his friends dared to ask him if his wife's conversation did not bother him just a little. "Oh, no,

I'm never put out by that," he replied. As a rejoinder to his
friend's observation that he "must be a man of extraordinary
qualities," Disraeli said, "Not at all; I only possess one quality
in which most men are deficient—gratitude." To somebody
else he said of his wife, "She believed in me when men
despised me."

He needed her belief and encouragement. For years he
struggled for advancement and the coveted cabinet post. Although a member of the Church of England and a professing
Christian, he still bore the reproach of a Hebrew ancestry.
And even though it was politically dangerous, he nevertheless
jumped to his feet in the House of Commons to protest a law
which kept a Jew from assuming the seat in Parliament to
which he had been elected.

Disraeli's appeal could not fail to stir the Christian conscience. In his speech he said, "Is it not the first business of
the Christian Church to make the population whose minds
she attempts to form, acquainted with the history of the Jews?
. . . On every sacred day you read to the people the exploits of
Jewish heroes, the proofs of Jewish devotion, the brilliant
annals of past Jewish magnificence. The Christian Church has
covered every kingdom with sacred buildings, and over every
altar . . . we find the tables of the Jewish law. Every Sunday,
if you wish to express feelings of praise and thanksgiving to
the Most High, or if you wish to find expression of solace in
grief, you find both in the words of the Jewish poets."

Disraeli concluded: "I cannot sit in this House with any
misconception of my opinion on this subject. Whatever may
be the consequences on the seat I hold, I cannot, for one, give
a vote which is not in deference to what I believe to be the
true principles of religion. Yes, it is as a Christian that I will
not take upon me the awful responsibility of excluding from

the legislature those who are of the religion in the bosom of which my Lord and Saviour was born."

Through all these years Mary Anne stood at his side. A debate in the House sometimes lasted until five o'clock in the morning. Mary Anne considered it her duty to give him a great welcome home. In the fireplace burned a welcoming fire, and the house was ablaze with lights. On occasions she waited in the carriage outside the House with a cold supper ready for him. Everything must minister to her beloved Dizzy.

That he was conscious of these ministries is seen in the inscription on the flyleaf of the book given to her. "I would inscribe these volumes to one whose noble spirit and gentle nature ever prompt her to sympathize with the suffering; to one whose sweet voice has often encouraged, and whose taste and judgment have ever guided, their pages; the most severe of critics, but—a perfect wife!"

Her Britannic Majesty Victoria had not always looked upon him with favor. When Stanley spoke about him, she had responded, "I do not approve of Mr. Disraeli." But his moment arrived when he became chancellor of the exchequer.

Although a personal financial failure, he was to oversee the finances of the greatest mercantile empire the world had ever known. He also had to make a daily report of the activities of the Commons to the queen. Gradually he worked his way into her affections. Of his reports she wrote, "Mr. Disraeli writes very curious reports, much in the style of his books."

But his era as chancellor was shortlived as the carousel of the British political system turned, bringing defeat to the government, leaving him to return again to the back benches of the house.

His real moment of triumph was long in coming, but finally Queen Victoria summoned him to request that he form a cabinet as prime minister of England. The queen had changed her mind about him now and extended her plump hand for him to kiss.

Mary Anne shared Disraeli's moment. She gave a reception at the Foreign Office. The weather outside was wretched with wind and rain; inside the reception was all glory and glitter. Mary Anne was escorted by the Prince of Wales, Dizzy had the Princess of Wales on his arm. For a month now Mary Anne had known she had cancer, but she did not wish to let Dizzy know. Nothing must mar his glorious hour. With typical humor he replied to the congratulations of his fellows, "I have climbed to the top of the greasy pole."

In another about-face of British politics, defeat came to Disraeli's party; and although entitled to request a place in the House of Lords, he thought only of Mary Anne. At his request she became Viscountess Beaconsfield while he remained Mr. Disraeli.

Mary Anne's title brought shortlived joy. Cancer took its toll, and she passed away September 15, 1872. She left a letter for him.

My Own Dear Husband,—If I should depart this life before you, leave orders that we may be buried in the same grave at whatever distance you may die from England. And now God bless you, my kindest, dearest! You have been a perfect husband to me. Be put by my side in the same grave. And now, farewell, my dear Dizzy. Do not live alone, dearest. Someone I earnestly hope you may find as attached to you as your own devoted

MARY ANNE

And in the eventide of life there was power again, as he became Prime Minister of England, and adulation and affection. As Maurois says, "No people are more sensitive than the English to the beauty wherewith time can adorn an object;

they love old statesmen, worn and polished by the struggle, as they love old leather and old wood."

A closeness with the widowed queen was such as no other statesmen had ever enjoyed. With the sense of dedication to the mystical monarchy, he brought her gifts, among them the title Empress of India and ownership of a controlling share of the Suez Canal. But it was of loved ones that they chatted, she of the beloved Prince Albert and he of Mary Anne. Each one, happily married for so long, cherished a happy and hallowed memory. Following his death the queen made the rare tribute of erecting a memorial to him.

TO

THE DEAR AND HONOURED MEMORY

OF

BENJAMIN EARL OF BEACONSFIELD

THIS MEMORIAL IS PLACED BY

HIS GRATEFUL SOVEREIGN AND FRIEND

VICTORIA R. I.

"Kings love him that speaketh right."

PROVERBS 16:13.

So much of Disraeli's world has gone. The beloved empire has slowly disappeared with its demise hastened by the island country's having poured out its blood in the mightiest war of history. India is now independent and torn in two and Suez has been lost.

Despite all the glamor of his day, Disraeli's greatest bequest may be the epic love of Mary Anne. The years that wrested

India and the Suez Canal brought a theory of complementary love needs which apparently fits the unlikely love affair of Dizzy and Mary Anne. Sometimes the inner emotional responses of man may be of greater importance than his moments of power and prestige.

5

Heart in Chitambo's Village

DAVID LIVINGSTONE (1813–1873)

There is ample evidence to show that David Livingstone ought never to have married. He obviously had doubts himself. When he applied to the London Missionary Society for missionary service, he said as much.

Filling out his application and answering a question about marriage, he candidly stated, "Unmarried, under no engagement relating to marriage, never made proposals of marriage, nor conducted myself so to any woman as to cause her to suspect that I intended anything relating to marriage; and, so far as my present wishes are concerned, I should prefer going out unmarried, that I might be without that care which the concerns of a family necessarily induce, and give myself wholly to the work." [1] Written in the flush of youthful enthusiasm, he little realized how prophetic were his words about family concerns.

His mother-in-law certainly had moments when she doubted the wisdom of the marriage, and many a malicious mind in England speculated as to how a husband ranging all over the countryside in Africa could remain loyal to a wife and family.

Livingstone had too many loves. Not women, mind you. Only one woman: Mary. But love is an object relationship. Livingstone loved exploration; he loved Africans; he loved to gather geological specimens, study the stars, the wonders of river formations; and he loved Jesus Christ.

Against such competition Mary had little hope.

I

Appropriately David's first glimpse of Mary should be of her traveling across the veldt in a wagon. Here father and mother, Robert and Mary Moffat, illustrious missionaries, had served valiantly for many years in Africa and now after a successful furlough in England were returning to their mission station in Kuruman.

Dr. David Livingstone, a young medical missionary, had come up the hard way. After commencing work in a factory at the tender age of nine, he had studied diligently in the evenings and finally took his medical degree and presented himself as a missionary candidate.

Traveling to Africa, he settled at first on Kuruman mission station, the normal home of the furloughing Moffats. Almost immediately he began his explorations of the surrounding country. By June, 1842, he had already traveled over a thousand miles. Thus early in his stay he had established the pattern of restless search.

At the time of the Moffat's return he had temporarily settled at a new station called Mabotsa, which literally means "marriage feast." It may be that the meaning of the name, added to loneliness of his life, put ideas in his head.

Livingstone had an air of drama about him. Mauled by a lion in his early African days, his injured arm hung awkwardly at his side as he rode up to the Moffat wagon to greet the returning missionary family.

He had come 150 miles to meet them, but with eyes only for Mary, who was to be known as the "Queen of the Wagon." No love-sick adolescent, at thirty years of age he had written to a friend and said, "There's no outlet for me when I begin to think of getting married but that of sending home an advertisement to the *Evangelical Magazine*, and if I get very old, it must be for some decent sort of widow. In the meantime I am too busy to think of anything of the kind." [2] The sight of Mary eliminated any thought of widows or advertisements.

He made contact with the Moffat family in the year 1844. After the meeting on the veldt he had gone to stay in their home. The picture of Mary Moffat in a domestic setting stirred something within this Scotsman. The practical nature of her religious conviction may also have attracted David to her; that there was no element of mysticism in it had been noted by Mary's mother.

Livingstone gives us a glimpse of his courtship in his own words, "After nearly four years of African life as a bachelor, I screwed up my courage and put a question beneath one of the fruit trees in Kuruman. . . ." [3] The almond tree had been planted by Mary's father. Sitting there Mary felt, as the Scotch say it, "a soft heart," for David.

Immediately after the engagement Livingstone was off to lonely Mabotso, where he wrote a letter to Mary, "And now, my dearest, farewell. May God bless you! Let your affection be towards Him much more than towards me; and, kept by his mighty power and grace, I hope I shall never give you cause to regret that you have given me a part. Whatever friendship we feel towards each other, let us always look to Jesus as our common friend and guide, and may He shield you with his everlasting arms from every evil!" [4] Mary was to discover the importance of the other Friend, of whom David spoke.

With characteristic enthusiasm Livingstone entered on the task of preparing a house for Mary. He both designed and built the house. While laboring on the building he tried to catch a falling stone and hurt his weak arm. The injury bothered him for the rest of his days. Perhaps this was symbolic of the disadvantages of married life for the missionary explorer.

No creature of stone, anticipation of marriage excited him. He wrote to a friend, "Let Moore, dear good fellow, know of my marriage. It will comfort all your hearts to know that I am becoming as great a fool as any of you. . . . In love! Words, yea thoughts, fail—so I leave it to your imagination and recollection. . . ." [5]

After all Livingstone's work in planning and building the new home and carefully planting the garden round about it, they did not enjoy it for long. An older colleague felt threatened by the younger man's enthusiasm and ability and voiced his misgivings that the youthful Livingstone should have a better home than he. In the following discussion Livingstone decided, in the interest of unity, to relinquish the house to his colleague. The newlyweds moved off and sorrowfully watched the deterioration of the garden they had so carefully planted and tended.

On the new station the young missionaries lost themselves in their work. Mary proved to be a worthy daughter of her illustrious parents. Livingstone describes her spending the morning in her domestic chores, the afternoon teaching school. He noted her popularity with the children. Laboring under difficult circumstances, she cared for anything up to eighty children, milked the cows and carried out special missionary ministries.

They named their first son Robert Moffat. He was the first of five children, who, in many ways, came to be both the joy and the despair of their father's life.

Livingstone suffered with itchy feet. The vast inland spaces of Africa forever called him on. Characteristically, with Mary and the ever-growing family struggling to stay by his side, he stepped out into the hinterland. The doctor-explorer delivered his children, rejoiced in each birth, but felt the restrictions they placed upon him.

In 1850 David delivered Mary of a daughter, their fourth child. In the midst of a raging epidemic, the child took ill and died at the age of six weeks. Loss of this baby affected Livingstone deeply, but he tried to be philosophical about it all. He wrote in his journal, "It was the first death in our family, but was just as likely to have happened had we remained at home, and we now have one of our number in heaven." [6] Some might have thought he was rationalizing.

Not only was there trouble with his baby but also with his wife. A serious illness left Mary with an unsightly paralysis of the right side of her face. David tried to nurse her back to health.

Then wagon wheels rolled again. David embarked on a fresh exploratory venture in April, 1851. His family accompanied him. Since their marriage the Livingstones had covered an incredible four thousand miles in their covered wagon.

When in October of 1851, Mary gave birth to her fifth child, the ever-growing uneasy feeling of years reached the point where Livingstone had to come to terms with it. He realized it would obviously not be possible for him to drag his family all over the unexplored jungles of Africa.

Mary's mother, Mrs. Moffat, had worried too over those nine years in which her daughter had hauled her family around Africa. She wrote a letter to Livingstone remonstrating with him about plans to take his wife and family with him on his future journeys. Mrs. Moffat's letter seemed like the last straw. So there came the reluctant decision to return to civilization.

Nine years after their marriage the Livingstones' wagon bumped down the rutted roadway to Cape Town. The family made a strange sight in their improvised and much repaired clothing, which one biographer notes was somewhat reminiscent of Robinson Crusoe.

Livingstone faced the question that must puzzle every missionary. It is one thing to volunteer for missionary service in the flush of youth, but what of wife and family in later days? Can children be raised in a foreign land? He felt so strongly about it that he took occasion to write a letter to the directors of his missionary society pointing up the difficulties confronting missionaries facing a decision about their children's education.

All in all, it seemed best that Mary take the children back to England where they could get their education; and on April 23, 1852, Mrs. Livingstone and the four surviving children set sail for England.

David Livingstone made it perfectly clear how much he felt the burden of separation.

Cape Town
May 5, 1852

My Dearest Mary,

How I miss you now, and the children! My heart yearns incessantly over you. How many thoughts of the past crowd into my mind! I feel as if I would treat you all much more tenderly and lovingly than ever. You have been a great blessing to me. You attended to my comfort in many, many ways. May God bless you for all your kindnesses! I see no face now to be compared with that sunburnt one which has so often greeted me with its kind looks. Let us do our duty to our Saviour, and we shall meet again. . . .'[7]

Mary and her children were destined to be separated from their husband and father for four years. Livingstone had his moments of depression. He wrote in September, 1852, "Am I on my way to die in Sebituane's country? Have I seen the end of my wife and children? The breaking up of all my connections with earth, leaving this fair and beautiful world, and knowing so little of it?"[8]

The years tried Mary. Born in Africa, she had spent her life on a mission station and was not really English. Perhaps in moments of bitterness she pondered it all. Why hadn't David been like a hundred other missionaries? Like her daddy, for example, who was willing to settle down at one station and spend his life in that one spot.

Mary's mother had never been entirely at home in England. How they had anticipated furlough, and then when it came it was almost an anticlimax. Mary Moffat had written to a friend, "I long for my own home, for though loaded with kindness of friends, and welcome everywhere, still home is homely." English born, her friends and relatives were there, but it wasn't really home.

The younger Mary had no home, only a wagon. "Queen of the Wagon," she had been called, but the ravages of the tropical climate and the bearing of five children in six years had taken their toll. Nothing very regal about her now in her drab little house.

She became more reserved and retiring, living among English people who were sometimes less than flattering as they spoke about individuals coming from "the colonies."

II

David Livingstone's arrival in England in 1856 after fifteen years in Africa was not unlike the triumphal return of a Roman emperor. At his chariot wheels he brought the fruits of exploration in "darkest Africa" and in his being personified the civilizing forces of the British Empire. Physician, minister of the gospel, scientist, explorer—a most unlikely combination, but one of which so many people could be proud.

Mary knew all this but to her he was, first of all, husband. She turned poet for the occasion. But the ship came in to the wrong berth, and they missed each other at the landing. David put everything to one side and raced to where she waited. Shyly she produced the verse upon which she had worked so long.

A hundred thousand welcomes, and it's time for you to come
From the far land of the foreigner, to your country and your
    home.
O long as we were parted, ever since you went away,
I never passed a dreamless night, or knew an easy day.
Do you think I would reproach you with the sorrows that I bore?
Since the sorrow is all over, now I have you here once more,
And there's nothing but the gladness, and the love within my
    heart,
And the hope so sweet and certain that again we'll never part.

. . . .

A hundred thousand welcomes! how my heart is gushing o'er
With the love and joy and wonder thus to see your face once
    more.
How did I live without you these long long years of woe?
It seems as if 'twould kill me to be parted from you now.
You'll never part me, darling, there's a promise in your eye;
I may tend you wile I'm living, you may watch me when I die;
And if death but kindly lead me to the blessed home on high,
What a hundred thousand welcomes will await you in the sky!

MARY [9]

Alas for her hopes. She had to share him. Everybody wanted to honor the intrepid explorer.

First there was the meeting of the Royal Geographical Society with a gathering of illustrious explorers and distinguished personalities. The presidential speech praised the work of Livingstone and climaxed a memorable utterance with the presentation of the Society's medal.

The man who had fought with lions, conquered rivers and mountains, and carved a track through the forests struggled to express himself in his native tongue. Rusty through disuse, his English didn't come easily but he managed to get his message across. A missionary, his work had only begun; a great continent must be opened to civilization and the gospel of Christ. The iniquitous slave trade must be abolished.

The very next evening saw the London Missionary Society paying its tribute in the Freemason's Hall. That great Christian Lord Shaftesbury presided. Appropriately the chairman paid tribute to Mary Livingstone. "That lady," he said, "was born with one distinguished name, which she had changed for another. She was born a Moffat, and she became a Livingstone. She cheered the early part of our friend's career by her spirit, her counsel, and her society. Afterward, when she reached this country, she passed many years with her children in solitude and anxiety, suffering the greatest fears for the welfare of her husband, and yet enduring all with patience and resignation, and even joy, because she had surrendered her best feelings, and sacrificed her own private interests, to the advancement of civilization and the great interests of Christianity." [10]

Friends and advisers pressed in on Livingstone. To make history imposed the obligation to record it. Livingstone had been meticulous in keeping his journal. Now came the offer from a publisher to produce a book.

Faced with the task of writing, Livingstone struggled with the problems of all new authors. The task so bothered him that he claimed it was the most difficult enterprise he had ever undertaken. He used to say he would rather cross Africa than write another book.

Sedentary life had no appeal to Livingstone, but this writing stint gave him one of the few periods of his life with his children. He did not even mind their shouts and noise. He developed a technique of concentrating his attention on his work and tuning out the intrusions of the childrens' voices.

Surrounded by manuscripts and journals, he made certain times to lay them aside and walk with his little brood or romp around the room. One biographer notes, "Busy though he was, this must have been one of the happiest times of his life."

Honors flooded to him. His book was an instant success. Cities bestowed their freedom upon him. But Africa called. When time came for him to leave, the presiding officer summed up the fruits of his visit, "Notwithstanding eighteen months of laudation, so justly bestowed on him by all classes of his countrymen, and after receiving all the honors which the Universities and cities of our country could bestow upon him, he is still the same honest, true-hearted David Livingstone as when he issued from the wilds of Africa." [11]

III

They planned the most elaborate expedition yet to explore to the Zambesi River. Mary stood at David's side again. She would accompany him along with Oswell, their youngest child.

Speaking of Mary, Livingstone praised her:

"It is scarcely fair to ask a man to praise his own wife, but I can only say that when I parted from her at the Cape, telling her that I should return in two years, and when it happened that I was absent four years and a half, I supposed that I should appear before her with a damaged character. I was, however, forgiven. My wife, who has always been the main spoke in my wheel, will accompany me in this expedition, and will be most useful to me. She is familiar with the languages of South Africa. She is able to work. She is willing to endure, and she well knows that in that country one must put one's hand to everything. In the country to which I am about to proceed she knows that at the missionary's station the wife must be the maid-of-all-work within, while the husband must be the jack-of-all trades without, and glad am I indeed that I am to be accompanied by my guardian angel." [12]

Livingstone struggled with his loves. His love of exploration could not be denied, but he was broken-hearted at the necessity of having to go without the other members of his family. He had faced up to the grim necessity of it all.

Better equipped than ever before, they took with them a steam launch to be assembled in Africa and used on the rivers to further their exploration efforts. They named the launch "Ma-Robert," Mrs. Livingstone's African name—another indication of the esteem in which David held his wife.

In spite of their hopes, Mrs. Livingstone became ill on the outward voyage. They reluctantly decided that she should be left at the Cape. Pregnant again, how she must have bemoaned her fertility. She hoped that having borne her child she would join her exploring husband once more. To a friend Livingstone wrote, "It was a bitter parting with my wife, like tearing the heart out of one."

A long time in coming, that reunion—not until 1859 did he receive the news that his wife had given birth to a little daughter on the 16th of November, 1858. The baby girl had been in the world for almost a year before her father knew of her existence.

Livingstone was writing history, preparing Africa, the sleeping giant, for its world-shattering awakening. He had his troubles, made his mistakes, but continued to add luster to his name.

Mary, having given birth to her child, had to make her decision. Where would she go?

To her husband sailing up the Zambesi River and now almost impossible of being joined?

She could remain with her parents. It was her home here in South Africa. Here too she was "the Queen of the Wagon." Fond parents would welcome her home.

Then there were the children in Scotland.

To Scotland she went for four miserable years of separation and bitterness.

Tongues began to wag. There were differences between them, they said. Her husband couldn't bear to live with her. Dr. Livingstone, following the example of so many white men, was involved in illicit relationships with native women.

Mary went through her Gethsemane.

IV

After four years in Scotland Mary could stand it no longer. She desperately wanted to be with her husband.

Livingstone for his part, knowing the rigors of the tropics, suggested they wait until he had found a healthy spot for building a house.

Mary, not to be denied, determined to join her husband. When the H.M.S. *Gorgon* after a difficult trip appeared off the Zambesi River, observers on Livingstone's boat, the Pioneer, watched the new arrival.

Signals ran up the mast of H.M.S. *Gorgon*, "I have a steamboat in the brig."

"Welcome news."

The message from the ship, "Wife aboard."

Livingstone replied, "Accept my best thanks."

The next day Livingstone's boat came out to take off the passengers.

Mary watched anxiously, straining her eyes as she fastened them on the puffing little paddle boat approaching the ship. There he stood; he looked robust and strong standing by the port paddle box issuing his short commands. He looked something like a naval officer, head covered by the gold-laced cap she knew had become so much a part of him.

"That is he," said Dr. Stewart at her elbow, and Mary, so ill and depressed on the voyage out, felt a new sense of joy at the prospect of reunion.

Livingstone was anxious to get his wife out of the delta so infamous for its fever. He communicated his anxiety to his father-in-law when he wrote, "Mary has, I am happy to say, joined me at last, after a weary and unexpected separation."

A few halcyon days followed. The reunion of David and Mary after so many years of separation was particularly satisfying. They spent much time together. Evenings were especially enjoyable as they walked the decks, went ashore, or sat around with the ship's officers.

Then fever. Slight touches at first, the prelude to a full-scale attack.

They took Mary ashore. David accompanied her and never left her side. After six days of illness she began to sink with sudden swiftness.

Perhaps it was symbolic, that crude hut, the primitive bed made of boxes and covered with a mattress. The physician husband anxiously feeling for the pulse of life found it gone. Tears flowed. A life surrounded by death had not prepared him for this passing.

Shaken by his inadequacy as a physician, perhaps with doubts about his effectiveness as a missionary, he turned to Dr. Stewart, "Please, please commit her soul to her Maker in prayer."

Livingstone's own words written in his journal best describe his reactions.

"It is the first heavy stroke I have suffered, and quite takes away my strength. I wept over her who well deserved many tears. I loved her when I married her, and the longer I lived with her I loved her the more. God pity the poor children who were all tenderly attached to her, and I am left alone in the world by one whom I felt to be a part of myself. I hope it may, by divine grace, lead me to realise heaven as my home, and that she has but preceded me in the journey. Oh my Mary, my Mary! how often we have longed for a quiet home, since you and I were cast adrift at Kologeng; surely the removal by a kind Father who knoweth our frame means that He rewarded you by taking you to the best home, the eternal one in the heavens. . . ." [13]

V

For ten more years Livingstone's work of exploration continued. The end came in his lonely camp as his native servant found him characteristically in a posture of prayer by his bed. No other white man was present.

It was a fitting climax that, having embalmed the body with salt and wrapped it in bark and sail cloth, sixty black men should have embarked on an eight-months journey to carry the body across Africa to the sea in what has been described as one of "the finest exploits in the whole history of travel."

The memorial stone in Westminster Abbey is inscribed, "Brought by faithful hands over land and sea here rests David Livingstone."

His body was laid to rest in Westminster Abbey but not his heart. The faithful natives had removed and buried his heart. It lay in Chitambo's Village. It was appropriately there in the land he loved.

6

Out of the Depths

ANTON T. BOISEN (1876–1965)

Considering woman, medieval man was torn in two directions. As the daughter of Eve, she personified for him the
temptress who had lured Adam from the pathway of right-
eousness, causing him to fall and be forever expelled from
paradise. But she had also descended from Mary, the Mother
of God, who made it possible for God to descend to earth in
the form of man to gain salvation for His fallen creatures.
Women had enticed man into the depths of hell and elevated
him to the heights of heaven.

One modern man followed a tenuous pathway descending
into the hell of psychosis and climbing to the heights of
spiritual experience and service to his fellow-man. The guiding

light he followed was carried by a daughter of Eve named
Alice and his name was Anton.

Anton T. Boisen would have agreed with the analysis and
examination of his life. Sensitive to an unusual degree, he was
almost painfully open and honest as he revealed some intimate and personal aspects of his own experience in his writings. He constantly urged upon students of personality the
importance of studying "the living document."

In many ways before his time, he occupied the first full-time
chaplaincy post in a mental hospital, and he fathered a unique
idea in theological education. Although his approach to religious experience was a scientific one, he nevertheless perceived
the shortcomings of an allegedly scientific stance which over-
looked the place of religion and values in psychotherapy.

My deeper interest in Anton T. Boisen was sparked when a
counselee gave me a copy of the autobiography *Out of the
Depths*. Although I had not considered those counseling sessions particularly successful, he was gracious enough to inscribe the book with my name, adding, ". . . who helped
bring me out of my depths."

In reading this unusual book, I was fascinated by the number of times Boisen referred to a woman who so profoundly
influenced him. It seemed that his love for Alice Batchelder
overshadowed all his experiences for a goodly portion of life.
Retracing my steps to read his preface, I happened upon a
statement in which Boisen admits that his autobiography is
really a love story which cannot be understood apart from
Alice Batchelder. This remarkable woman had agreed with
him that the story of their unusual relationship should be told;
and he concedes that she might have illuminated many a
mysterious event, but an untimely death snatched her away.

Boisen laments that in many ways the relationship is a

tragedy. Tragedy it is, but with a difference. It is not the sordid story of promiscuity, unfaithfulness or illegitimacy. Rather it is the tragedy of the tormented struggle of a sensitive spirit, forever reaching toward an elusive love object with a zeal continuing unabated across the years. The untimely death of Alice brought little respite. Her memory, like a haunting ghost, continued to flit across the pathway of the aging Boisen.

I

The story begins in the time-honored manner of all love literature with the lover's idealization of his beloved. It was love at first sight. Memories of that encounter long lingered in Boisen's mind.

Sitting among the students in a college convocation, Boisen looked closely at the twenty-two year old girl. Above average in height, she carried herself with what he liked to call a queenly bearing. A halo of wavy golden hair crowned her finely featured face. After the chairman introduced her to the students, Alice Batchelder spoke in reply. He never could remember what she said—the words slipped away from him—but the tones of that clear, well-modulated voice conveyed the sincerity and earnestness of the attractive young woman.

He knew he had fallen in love. Completely and unreservedly. Though she knew it not, as Alice spoke that day, she swept Boisen off his feet.

Seen through Boisen's eyes, Alice was an angel who could do no wrong. The uninvolved observer might have concluded otherwise. To the onlooker's eyes she seems priggish and prudish, aloof to an unusual degree. She treated Boisen's doglike devotion with disdain and rejection, sometimes almost cruel derision. Yet when he mustered enough courage to throw down his ultimatum to finish it all, she dropped her tiny morsels of encouragement. Not unlike the alcoholic's wife who loudly protests his drinking habits but periodically spikes his drinks to keep him dependent on her, Alice apparently enjoyed the pursuit of Anton.

Unlike many of the great lovers who were really early adolescents, Boisen and Alice were both in their early twenties. They had reached an age when they could make a mature judgment.

Some critics of romantic love claim that differences foster the experience but that without an adequate basis of shared interests there is little hope for anything like a permanent relationship. Not so for Boisen and Alice—they shared many an interest, and the aspiring lover made the most of their common love of nature.

Although Anton took advantage of every opportunity to see Alice, he found her elusive. As rapidly as he thought up reasons for them to be together, she deftly countered with excuses. Nature's awakening in spring brought new hope for him. He knew the location of many of the choice parts of the countryside that had burst into a glorious carpet of arbutus. Nature-loving Alice could not resist the allure and joined him on trips of exploration.

An excursion to Cedar Bluff provided his moment. Ostensibly they had gone to search for shooting star and columbine, but as they stood admiring the delicate flowers, Anton plucked up his courage to stammer out his love for Alice. A dismal silence followed his declaration, and sensing the lack of response, he changed his plea and asked Alice for her friendship.

Very gently, yet firmly, Alice told the disappointed Anton that she had no love for him, and that friendship would carry an implication of a possibility for it to develop into something deeper. Alice let it be known she considered it best that they terminate the relationship.

So they parted, and the disappointed Boisen later learned that Alice had accepted a YWCA position in Missouri and had departed for that distant state.

Such an unpromising start might have daunted a lesser man, but it only stimulated greater desire in Boisen. Following through on his interests in forestry, he worked that summer in Maryland forests and spent the days with Alice constantly on his mind as he counted rings of bald cypress and loblolly pine.

Boisen's ever-active imagination kept him in a state of constant turmoil with youthful sexual thoughts flitting across the screen of his mind. In his despair he finally concluded he would not contact Alice again until he had his sexual thought-life under control.

After a three-month period of struggle in which he felt he had at last gained the victory, he took his pen in hand to write to Alice telling of his continued interest. The lady did not deign to reply, thus confirming she was through with it all.

With the completion of his first year in Yale's Forestry School, Boisen requested an assignment in New Hampshire, which happened to be Alice's native state. He received the appointment and after his stint of service decided to surprise Alice by stopping off at her town and calling on her. Alas for his hopes, the surprise visit didn't impress her, and he met with a chilly reception. By his own account it left him "heartbroken" and he decided to bury himself in his forestry work.

In his despondency Boisen passed through a period of turmoil which led him to conclude that he must write and tell Alice of his moral struggle and of his decision to study forestry. Finishing the letter, he turned to his Bible. As a liberal Bible student and a scientific investigator, Boisen had no use for superstition but, on the verge of a great decision, he sought

guidance by opening his Bible at random and chanced upon
the verse, "Then said he to the disciple, 'Behold thy mother'"
(John 19:27). To the confused man this seemed a tremendous revelation. Overwhelmed by the message, he concluded
that in his relationship with Alice, his love for her was a
reaching out to some stronger person and in reality a desperate
cry for salvation.

His call to the ministry came in an equally unusual manner.
It overwhelmed him with its suddenness. Walking down
Chapel Street, it seemed for a moment that he had been
snatched away and dropped into the countryside. Hills, trees,
flowers and more flowers—in luxuriant abundance they covered the hillside. He had found them at last. He must show
others where the flowers grew.

A clumsy pedestrian bumped him back to reality, to a
reality which found him dazed and confused. He recalled how
his father loved to search for wild flowers and concluded that
was the key to his vision.

Father? What of Alice? Was it not with her that he had
searched for wild flowers? And even as he saw the flowery hills
beckoning in a call to a life of ministry guiding others, there
came the consciousness that he might have a dedicated fellow
worker named Alice.

On the following day he wrote two letters to Alice telling
her of his decision for the ministry and confessing the hope
that they might serve together. Following a third letter, Alice
at last replied with a communication which was nothing if not
frank. She told him of her distress at the hinted proposal in his
letters and urged him not to write or think of her anymore. A
barb in the latter part of the communication reminded him
that a man's love for God must always be higher than his love
of a woman and that this was the only worthy motive for the
man of God.

The disappointing response sent Boisen's world crashing

around him. He succumbed to the sexual fantasy which worried him so much and wondered if he would ever be the person he longed to be.

Following the close of the school year in 1905, Boisen entered the United States Forest Service. Thus he began an exciting and interesting career as part of the rapidly burgeoning conservationist movement which, encouraged by President Theodore Roosevelt, was moving forward with immense strides. But two years of work and travel, although interesting and rewarding, could not erase the memory of Alice nor the possibility of serving God in some special way. He paid off the indebtedness he had incurred in the forestry course and then felt he must decide whether to continue in forestry or return to his "call to the ministry."

The chance hearing of a sermon on the subject of the "Broken Vessel" rekindled Boisen's desire to enter the ministry. As on so many other occasions, he sat down and addressed himself to Alice, telling her of his confusion in trying to decide on a career. Alice had been rejected as a missionary volunteer, and this disappointment may have softened her. She agreed to see him.

They met at the Baptist Training Institute in Philadelphia early in the winter of 1908. The chill of the evening was descending upon them, and Anton moved as if in a dream as they sat and talked together. Alice maintained a tight control of the situation; in a kind but firm manner she carefully guided the conversation and allowed him to speak only of the subjects which she approved.

What he would have done to prolong that session, but Alice brought it to a conclusion by offering a prayer and in it asking God's wisdom and guidance for Anton. The whole episode had the overtones of a mother carefully guiding the experiences of her immature child. Anton struggled within himself but could not hold back the tears that streamed down his face.

Then with the deliberate calmness he so much admired, but at this moment detested, she stretched forth her hand for a farewell handshake. Plucking up his courage he took her hand, bent over, and tenderly and with obvious emotion kissed it several times.

The warmth of his lips and the sight of his tears moved Alice for a moment. She struggled, then gaining fresh aplomb, she said, "God's promises always come true."

II

Conscious of new accessions of strength and a feeling of well-being, the would-be minister made his plans to become a student at Union Theological Seminary the following fall. Like a moth drawn to the flame, his thoughts turned again to Alice, and he composed a letter to her referring to the words with which she had concluded their last meeting. He interpreted these as a promise and told her he would never accept from her anything she could not give freely.

Her prompt response clarified the situation. She made it perfectly clear that no promise had been given; if he had gained such an impression, he completely misunderstood the situation. Boisen reacted by succumbing to a period of turmoil and confusion which lasted until he entered the seminary.

Seminary life opened up for Boisen what he came to consider as the three happiest years of his life. The new period of study commenced with a joyful omen. Alice consented to renew their correspondence.

During his second year in seminary he became engrossed in his studies although Alice was never really far from his mind, but when she made the rather unromantic suggestion that they correspond in French, he found it difficult to enter into the arrangement with any sort of enthusiasm. Moreover, Alice wrote her letters on her official stationery which Boisen saw as a discouraging sign.

The one bright gleam in the gathering gloom came in the end of his second year of seminary life when Alice sent him her picture. This portrait became one of his most treasured possessions.

Christmas of 1910 found Boisen filled with joy and expectation. Not only the yuletide affected him. Alice had come to visit the seminary. He accompanied her to Lowell, Massachusetts. They went to hear the symphony on what he described as "one memorable evening." The following day, while walking to a nearby town, she told him no other man had a place in her life and that she had decided to give her heart a chance. As promising as all this sounded, she explained she wasn't committing herself, but the buoyant hope left Boisen walking on air as he returned to seminary life.

His approaching graduation brought with it a period of conflict in which he faced a problem common to many seminary graduates as he contemplated the possibility of finding a church. The situation was further aggravated by his conviction that Alice should share the pastorate with him.

Taking advantage of their common interest in wild flowers, Boisen wrote to her proposing that as soon as the arbutus bloomed they might visit some of the spots they knew from bygone days. Alice upset his carefully laid plans when she wrote at the last minute to inform him she had made other arrangements and planned to visit a closer spot at Ponemah, New Hampshire. He could join her but a girl friend would also accompany them.

That momentous day, if Boisen, later looking back on the event, correctly interpreted the situation, Alice awaited his proposal. Her friend discreetly left them alone, but not before she gave Boisen a broad hint by telling him Alice looked like a bride surrounded by all those flowers. His moment had at last arrived.

But Alice's veto of his original plans had bothered him. In his confusion about it all he capitulated to his sexual weakness and now felt thoroughly demoralized.

Faced with the opportunity he had hoped for across the years, some maddening force kept him from speaking. He fought a battle within himself. What should he say? How should he do it?

In his embarrassment he suggested that he take Alice's picture. He had her take up a pose, then another and another. So he continued on until he had exposed a whole roll of film. Then the friend returned and he stood with his twelve pictures but having failed to grasp the chance for which he had waited so long.

How frequently he recalled this lost moment of opportunity we do not know, but even in the last words of his autobiography he recollects the peculiar pain surrounding that event at Ponemah. Thoroughly confused in his relationship with Alice, Boisen stumbled into one blunder after another.

After his return to the seminary he wrote begging for the privilege to see her again. Alice's reply informed him that she did not intend to meet him again unless she felt that she could really give him her love.

"Unless I can really give you my love"—how those words haunted him. He evaluated and reevaluated Alice. Now that he had missed her and been cut off from a relationship with her, all her strong points stood out in vivid clarity. He knew she had a high temper and admired her for the way she kept it under control. He marvelled that she followed the dictates of her conscience no matter how she felt. In that moment he recollected her unusual abilities in both painting and writing. What a remarkable wife and mother she would have made.

III

Boisen went back to his studies and his work. The memory of Alice remained with him, and at Christmas in 1911, she once again agreed to let him correspond with her. Boisen mentioned in one of his letters that he was taking a church. Alice's reply had a coquettish tone as she let it slip that she was very skillful at "keeping house and making pancakes." Boisen, not unnaturally, took this as an opening and hastened to present her with an opportunity to share his parsonage as his bride. In a steaming response she said she had never loved him. Her answer had been given and could not be changed.

In his disappointment Boisen buried himself in his work. He had been called as pastor of an unusual church in Wabaunsee, Kansas. Behind the church's unorthodox name lay a fascinating story. It was built by a group of settlers who traveled from New Haven to Kansas in 1857. To the desire to settle a new part of the country, they added the zeal of devoted fighters against slavery. These abolitionists were determined to save the state of Kansas from the curse of slavery, and they went forward with the prayers and well-wishes of fellow abolitionists. Before leaving New Haven, Henry Ward Beecher's church had given each church member a Bible and a Sharpe's rifle to provide them both spiritual and carnal weapons with which to face their foes. The history of the church was perpetuated in their name: The Beecher Bible and Rifle Church.

With remarkable enthusiasm Boisen threw himself into the leadership of his church and showed the value of his wide training and experience by leading out in a host of community projects. But fine traditions and a progressive spirit don't always go together, and after two years he reached the frustrating conclusion that his usefulness as minister of the church had come to an end.

A sense of failure troubled the young minister, and despite the urgings of friends towards a career in social work, he felt he should redeem himself "in Alice's eyes."

A call to a new church followed; here his ministry met with a measure of success that helped to rescue him from a sense of total failure. While in both churches he had attempted to contact Alice but with no response.

American entry into World War I gave Boisen an opportunity to serve overseas as a YMCA secretary. Although separated by miles he constantly thought of Alice. They did not correspond, but Boisen kept track of her activities through all his time abroad.

Returning eagerly from his overseas stint in 1919, Boisen's first thoughts turned to Alice; and he sought to visit her in her Chicago home. Alice refused to see him. He continued to write to her but with no response.

Boisen was nothing if not persistent. When he had an opportunity to serve with the Congregation Social Service Commission, his mind turned immediately to his beloved Alice. Would she be a partner in this new enterprise? He contacted her and eagerly awaited her reply.

A letter dated June, 1920, brought a welcome invitation from Alice to call on her as he passed through Chicago on his way back east. Not exactly a hearty invitation this. She told him of her misgivings as to whether he should come and laid down the condition that he not try to see her alone. She would be with her family, which included her sister Anne, and a friend Miss Catherine Wilson.

Anton readily accepted the conditions and right on the dot

at 6:30 presented himself at the apartment door. Nine years had flown since last they met, and he inwardly speculated as to what time had done with the woman he loved.

He later wrote in his diary that there were changes in her but only the changes he would have wished to find in a woman he prized above every other he had ever met.

They sat and talked as a group and Anton loved every moment, clinging desperately to a hope that some strange move of fate might give them an opportunity to have a few moments together. But it was not to be. And when he smiling told the company he hoped they would invite him to return again, Alice made sure that her whole demeanor shouted a refusal.

IV

Let Alice beware. Another love object appears on the horizon. A most unlikely object discovered in a most improbable setting.

The experience overwhelmed him, struck him down, imprisoned him, yet it provided the most rewarding insights in all his life. He toppled into his most serious psychotic episode.

Committed to a mental hospital, he remained a patient for fifteen months. In his own perception on the experience he claimed the whole episode centered on his "love affair." But apparently Alice made no move to visit or in any way offer her help.

Writing about the experience in his autobiography, Boisen heads the chapter "A Little Known Country." In that no man's land he observed it all so clearly that he charted much of this hazy area of human experience and wrote of it with great lucidity in his *Exploration of the Inner World.* Few persons have ever spoken with such authority and clarity about the shady borderland of psychosis.

When at last the clouds began to lift, Boisen discovered it is sometimes easier to get into a mental hospital than to get out. Feeling the need for action, he gave himself to organizing activities for the patients. The idea of training ministers in a closer understanding of the problems of the mentally ill was probably born here.

Following his discharge in January, 1922, he plunged into his many interests. A growing conviction led Boisen to believe he should devote his life to working in mental hospitals. While preparing for his work, he wrote a report of his experiences during hospitalization. He naturally sent copies of the document to his beloved Alice.

April 17, 1922, found him writing a long letter to Alice. In it he described a day which he had spent in the woods at the identical spot they had visited eleven years before. In a moving manner he told how he had sat in the same station and recalled how they had sat there, how he had wandered among the flowers as when with her and felt the nearness of her spirit. He gathered great armfuls of flowers. Sitting on the warm earth, he sorted out the choicest blooms and packed them in damp moss, taking the box back to the station to mail the flowers to her.

Gathering the flowers was indeed love's labor lost. Because of a moth infestation the entire region was in quarantine. Boisen contemplated circumventing the regulation by mailing the flowers in Boston, but his conscience would not let him do it. So he had sent them to his mother instead. The letter to Alice ended with an assurance that although he sent no flowers she could be assured of the constancy of both his thoughts and his love.

The other love of Boisen's life, a ministry to the mentally ill, went on unabated. By stretching meager financial resources his studies continued. At Harvard, Dr. Cabot's seminar on preparing case records proved to be one of the best he'd ever taken. Professor McDougal's teaching focused on theories of mind and body. Work in psychometrics under Dr. Frederick Lyman Wells left him with doubts about the value of intelligence-measuring procedures. But he found his most satisfying work in the social service department, which gave him access to case study material where he could study total man and his environment.

He had spent much time preparing a plan for research into the relationship of religion and mental illness. He had hoped that the National Committee for Mental Hygiene would sponsor the project but after early encouragement and almost interminable delays, they rejected the plan. Nevertheless, the moment of disappointment was tempered with the news that Dr. Bryan, medical superintendent of the Worcester State Hospital, was willing to try using a chaplain at his hospital.

As high as were Boisen's hopes as he entered upon this chaplaincy work, they were to be outdistanced by his ultimate accomplishments and those of the new movement to which his work gave birth.

Whatever role ministers had played in hospital life before that time had been limited and peripheral. Boisen entered on his new work with the clear understanding that he was to have no responsibility for recreation, library, or other administrative tasks. Anxious to have a correct professional status, one condition of his coming to the mental hospital was that as chaplain and research worker he should be able to visit patients on all the wards, attend staff meetings, have access to case records, and a recognition of his place as a member of the healing team.

One activity destined to have a long-lasting result was the young chaplain's compilation of a hymnal to be used by hospital patients. Boisen felt that the words of hymns might influence religious beliefs more than sermons. He had long noticed that the type of imagery used in some hymns had associations which could easily upset the psychotic patient. The hymns he chose were bound into a selection known as *Hymns of Faith and Courage*, the hymnbook still widely used in mental hospitals.

With fortitude far above the ordinary, Boisen continued to write a letter to Alice each week. Now that he had a definite plan for his ministry he sensed a new opportunity to ask the question never far from his mind. He wrote a letter asking if she might share life with him in his chaplaincy work.

Alice's reply left no room for misunderstanding. In what seems like a rather harsh response, she expressed shock that he should have interpreted her willingness to let him write as an indication of a deeper interest in him. There was absolutely no possibility of such a relationship, and she further indicated that because of the possibility of misunderstanding she was now withdrawing her previous permission to write.

With gentle patience Boisen wrote a long letter explaining that he could never cease corresponding with her even though she could not give him the answer he wanted. When she failed to respond to this letter, he resumed his letter-writing practices.

The rebuttal apparently added to his zeal and he penned a daily account of his happenings, mailing it each week to his beloved Alice. Hopes mounted as he wrote, but when he passed through Chicago in the spring of 1925, Alice refused to see him.

At this period Boisen introduced an innovation which might well be the most decisive single breakthrough in theological education in modern times. It came later to be referred to as clinical pastoral education.

The work of the doctors fascinated Boisen, and he felt that medical educators could teach the theological educator. He observed that the interns worked closely with both their teachers and the patients and that in the experience were exposed to the raw material of life.

It seemed to him that this had a special meaning for theological education. Students for the ministry should spend less time in laboriously studying books and more with what he called the "human documents" of a mental hospital. He concluded that a clinical experience was just as important for the minister charged with caring for the souls of men as it was for the doctor responsible for their bodies.

The plan calls for a theological student to work directly with people in trouble, generally in some institutional setting, and to write "verbatims" (word-by-word accounts of his experiences). These are then discussed with the chaplain supervisor under whose guidance he works. In the process the student learns to work as part of the healing team, gains skills in helping others, and learns about his own personality and relationships to life. The movement has spread, and it has been estimated that over 2500 ministers in the United States have participated in such clinical training programs.

The fall of 1926 presented an opportunity for Boisen to do a semester's teaching in seminary. Preparation of material and contacts with the professors proved to be very stimulating and provocative, but the proximity of the seminary to Alice's home may have been at least a contributing factor in making his decision to accept the position. If such hopes existed they were in vain. Alice still refused to see him. Boisen continued to write.

Did he finally see the futility of it all? Despite every discouragement across the years, Boisen had continued to hope and write, but now it seems he'd had enough. He mustered his courage, and on Christmas day of 1926 he took pen in hand to write the most difficult letter of all to Alice. He reminded her of the influence she had so long exercised over him and told her that he had now decided the time had come to end a one-sided relationship. This would be his last letter. In the closing lines of the letter he again reaffirmed that he loved and needed her but realized at last it must end.

The romance of Anton and Alice had concluded.

Thus it might fittingly have finished, but his attachment to Alice was too strong. That love would not let him go and continued to tantalize and torture his troubled spirit. Although he busied himself in a multiplicity of fascinating activities his mind turned to her again and again.

V

The 2nd of June, 1928, found Boisen greatly excited as he anticipated what he considered to be an occasion of the greatest significance. Nine months after he had laid down his ultimatum and finished it all Alice sent him a birthday card.

January of 1928 brought a reply to his letter and communication was gradually reestablished. Now after not having seen each other for eight years, they were to meet again. Alice was apprehensive; Anton, excited. They met in Chicago at Marshall Field's, and Boisen notes he did not have the slightest difficulty in recognizing her. They went to the Palmer House for lunch.

A new comfortable companionship came into existence. For a period of time they continued to see each other with luncheons downtown, and sometimes attended a play or an opera. Apparently their relationship moved on a purely platonic level.

A great event took place on Thanksgiving day of 1929. When Anton arrived to pick Alice up for their evening out, he brought a corsage of tiny roses. Alice received them with genuine delight. In the course of the evening, they wandered into the Hilton Chapel. The beautifully furnished little sanctuary exerted its influence upon them, and Anton suggested they kneel at the altar while he prayed. That stammering prayer brought a hush over them both, and tears moistened Alice's eyes as they rose to leave.

The following day brought Anton a letter which sent his spirits soaring. In it Alice told him how his prayer had affected her and that the little roses now in water on the table were a continuing reminder of their covenant. She confessed that for the first time in all the years she had known him she could honestly sign "with real affection."

At last, after twenty-seven years of discussion, Alice was really ready to do something about regularizing their relationship. She now had committed herself to a covenant of friendship and was able to sign "with real affection."

November of 1930 saw Boisen slipping into another psychotic episode. Alice, at the heart of it all, seems to have made no effort to contact him.

Following his recovery Boisen accepted the position of chaplain at the Elgin State Hospital in Illinois. One reason for this move was obviously a desire to be close to the home of Alice Batchelder. The first day of April, 1932, saw him installed in Elgin, and the following summer he began one of his characteristic training programs with a group of students.

The last episode, if there was ever to be a last episode, came on August 24, 1935, with the most tragic of all letters from

Alice. It informed him that she was to undergo surgery. With admirable spirit she requested no visitors and no flowers. Boisen discovered to his horror that she had terminal cancer.

Strange thoughts crossed through his mind. How often he had disappointed her, what a mix-up their relationship had been, he had caused it all. And the demands he had made upon her. Now she was slipping away to leave him.

His book *The Exploration of the Inner World* was about to go to press. He dedicated it to his beloved Alice. It seems as if Boisen was about to topple into a psychosis again. He was able to stand off objectively and look at it and feel that in it he found the clarification for his relationship with Alice.

A tragedy—this is how Boisen himself described the epic love affair of his life. In the closing pages of his autobiography, he balances the tragedy against the gains.

Recalling the "might have been," he says that if Alice had yielded to his entreaties to become his wife he might have become a passably successful minister. If Boisen made a correct evaluation of Alice's capacities, she was a woman of rare ability. Skillful at writing and painting, he felt she would have presided over a home of the highest order. Might she have even eclipsed Boisen himself? Is it possible he could have gone down in history's record as Alice Boisen's husband?

Boisen's insights into the relationship of religious experience and mental illness have been evaluated by Hiltner. "For the long-run understanding treatment and prevention of mental illness and despite its apparent simplicity, it may well prove to be the twentieth century's most significant insight on this subject." Mowrer, research psychologist of the University of Illinois says of Boisen's *Exploration of the Inner World*, "This is one of the most profound documents of our time. . . . It was twenty years before its time."

Boisen himself, having looked it all over dispassionately,

decided that apart from his ill-fated love affair with Alice, there would have been no new light upon the interrelatedness of mental disorder and religious experience.

Nor would there have been the new element in theological education. Clinical pastoral education, a program which took trainee ministers out of the dusty libraries of theological schools and thrust them into the sea of human need in clinic, hospital, and penitentiary, came from Boisen. Study of the living, human documents has revolutionized the whole field of theological education. Boisen, happily married in his well-ordered home, might have satisfied his thirst for knowledge by organizing social surveys or investigating church organization, but he tells us in his own biography there probably would have been no clinical pastoral training movement.

Boisen's lost love was humanity's greatest gain. He lived his lonely life of bachelorhood and spent his retirement days living in the Elgin Hospital, where he died at the age of eighty-nine. No estimate of his life could ever be made without considering his dedication of the *Exploration of the Inner World.*

TO THE MEMORY OF A. L. B.

For her sake I undertook the adventure out of which this book has grown. Her compassion upon a wretch in direst need, her wisdom and courage and unswerving fidelity have made possible the measure of success which may have been achieved. To her I dedicate it in the name of the Love which would surmount every barrier, and bridge every chasm and make sure the foundations of the universe.

7

The Syndrome
of Romantic Love

Let linguists struggle with gobbledygook and mishmash, tongue twisters and esoteric terms; one little four-letter word can put most of these in the shade. The word *love* has such subtle nuances and overtones that its definition can baffle the most erudite student of the English language.

One way to attack this problem is to see the word *love* not as describing one single something but as an umbrella term concerning a number of different types of internal reactions and overt behaviors. An examination of eight of these may help to throw light on the strange contradictions of the experience that so frequently falls the lot of man.

(1) *Love is a dramatic and often unexpected experience which suddenly overtakes its victim...*

"He took her soft lily-white hand in his and looked down into the depths that were her eyes. His heart was racing madly.

He said, 'Why fight it? It is greater than both of us.' So they fell in love."

The reader of the stories of love and romance has a growing feeling that falling in love may be something like falling down a hole. As Alice in Wonderland slipped down an opening in the ground and found herself in a strange and mystifying new world, so the lover expects to enter a heightened new wonderland in which the grim realities of life will be of little significance. And the adventures of Alice at the Mad Hatter's tea party, as ludicrous as they may seem, are nothing when compared with the antics of some people who "fall in love."

An even more appropriate analogy might be to see the lover as being like a hunter. Pursuing his beloved, he stalks through the jungle of life. Then suddenly he "falls" into a trap in which his foot is caught in a noose which releases a bamboo tree which springs upright and suspends him dangling by his leg, as a spectacle for all to behold.

Holden Caulfield, representing a contemporary adolescent in J. D. Salinger's novel *Catcher in the Rye*, describes his experience: "I apologize like a madman because the band was starting a fast one. She started jitterbugging with me—but just nice and easy, not corny. She was really good. She knocked me out. I mean it. I was about half in love with her by the time we sat down." Later he went through the cycle again: "Finally Sally started coming up the stairs, and I started down to meet her. She looked terrific. She really did. She had on this black coat and sort of black beret. She hardly ever wore a hat, but that beret looked nice. The funny thing is, I felt like I was in love with her and wanted to marry her."

The irony of the situation is that although "falling in love" is the most commonly used expression to describe a love involvement, many impartial observers doubt whether there is such an experience as "falling in love." The infatuation so easily described as "falling in love" may in reality be one of the most unreal and unhealthy aspects of romantic love. Every great experience in life has a counterfeit and an imitation. Infatuation is the counterfeit of love. The sudden intense overwhelming experience with an inappropriate love object is frequently short-lived, leaving its subject disillusioned and frustrated.

As Karl Menninger says it, "We do not fall in love, we grow in love and love grows in us." Like some hothouse plant giving its short brilliant display only to wither quickly away, it lacks the time and testing of a long period of association to form the basis for a good relationship.

(2) *Being "in love" may distort the judgment of the individual.* The experience of romantic love is often accompanied by euphoria. The ecstasy of "being in love" causes the subject to look at the world through rose-colored glasses.

Eliza, the celebrated twenty-seventh wife of Brigham Young, tells of her reaction when at twenty-two years of age she met James Leech Dee: "The chance meeting soon ripened into a friendship and that into a near relationship. My whole life was brightened by the new sweet glory that swept in such a torrent upon me. It took on a new look and even the most common things were invested with a strange, novel interest. Nothing seemed natural. Everything in my life had deepened and broadened in the light of my new experience. Commonplace people grew interesting, commonplace events stirring. The whole world was tinted with the rose color of my romance. I was very happy."

The note of realism came later when a short time after their marriage Dee took a second wife. Eliza revolted and could not bear to have him near her and finally sought a divorce. Eliza's

life finished on a tragic note. She lived secluded and miserable in an existence as far removed from the early euphoria as
could be imagined.

Reik claims the last serious study of love was made over 150
years ago by the French novelist and essayist, Stendhal. This
serious student of the subject puzzled over the distortions of
romantic love.

Stendhal used a parable to make his point. In the salt mines
of Hallein near Salzburg, miners threw dead limbs of trees
into unused salt caverns. When later recovered the dead wood
was encrusted with brilliant crystals.

Stendhal described a visit to these mines with a party of
people which included a Germany army officer and an Italian
girl. The officer, attracted to the Italian, spent much time
talking about her. Stendhal was "most amazed by the air of
madness which pervaded the reflections of the officer; he was
incessantly finding in this woman perfections unseen by me."
The woman's hand had been disfigured in childhood, but the
perplexed Stendhal discovered that the soldier saw the girl's
hand as particularly beautiful.

Pondering the problem of the lover's seeing nonexistent
qualities in his beloved, Stendhal concluded much romantic
love was like the process of crystallization which changed the
dead wood into a sparkling jewel. Stendhal went on to postu-
late four stages in the process, (1) admiration, (2) the place
of feeling—"What a joy to be loved by that charming
woman," (3) the birth of hope, and (4) the stage of delight
in the beauty and merits of the love object. The latter Stendhal calls crystallization.

In almost all the writings on romantic love, the lover has a
misperception, overevaluates his beloved, and speaks of her in
heightened language. Casanova's biographer tells of a typical
reaction when he met Christina. "He was astonished, en-

chanted. Her silken dress, her jewelry, her figure, feet and
ankles; her walk, her free movements, her charming glance
. . . a princess in disguise." It is worthy of note that his
experience and rapture with Christina only lasted a few days.

The process is sometimes called idealization and is generally
part of a romantic experience. Unfortunately it may create
undue expectations which inevitably lead to disillusionment.

(3) *Love is a never-ending quest with the love object always
evading the lover's grasp.* Boccaccio's *Decameron* is said to be
"the supreme work of Italian prose," and one of the "master-
pieces of world literature." In it, Boccaccio, who loomed beside Petrarch as a great literary figure of the Renaissance, tells
the story of a group of seven girls and three men seeking
refuge from the plague which swept Italy in the fourteenth
century. The group took shelter on a country estate and
agreed that on ten successive days each would tell a story,
making one hundred stories in all. The stories are of great
variety, but all tell of some type of love experience.

Much of Boccaccio's inspiration is owed to a love affair of
his youth. Maria d' Aquina, educated in a convent, had married the Count of Aquina at age fifteen. A succession of lovers
followed; but when she appeared at mass on Holy Saturday in
1331, Boccaccio saw her for the first time and was immediately smitten. With her blonde hair and roguish eyes, she
seemed to him the fairest of the fair. He called her Fiametta,
"little flame," and like a moth he fluttered around in grave
danger of getting his wings singed.

For months Boccaccio did nothing but plot and plan to be
near her. His only reason for going to church was to catch a
glimpse of the "little flame." He walked up and down in the
street beneath her window; and when he heard she had gone
to Baiae, he hurried off to that city.

He took his pen in hand to write, but in everything Fiametta's influence made itself felt. Just as the wreckers on the British shoreline moved their lights in the darkened night to lure the mariners on to an apparent port of safety, but in reality to the cruel rocks, so the "little flame" ever flickered before him. At one and the same time she inspired his creativity and clouded his judgment. His jealousy caused him to write a poem which became the model for Chaucer's Knight's Tale, and in his psychological novel he made an effort to portray his misery through Fiametta's alleged autobiography in which she confessed Boccaccio had jilted her.

In the typical climax of the tale of romantic love, after seeking her for five years she became his and the affair died. An elusive will-o'-the-wisp, she could never really be caught and held.

The evasive element of romantic love is the reason Rougemont thinks romantic love and marriage are incompatible. Marriage brings certainty, and so the quest has come to an end, leaving the relationship colorless and insipid.

This factor may account for the attention of the illicit in romantic love. While "affairs" on the side in marriage are enticing, if the marriage is ruptured in divorce and the illicit relationship then normalized in marriage, it is very seldom successful. Apparently the spirit of the chase is lost. Instead of being the pursuer, the seducer has become the captive.

Like the modern western, innocuous and uninteresting without a fight and a chase, romantic love also must have as its main ingredient the process of pursuit, with the capture and possession somewhat anticlimactic.

(4) *Being in love is preeminently an experience of the emotions.* There is no more unprofitable and frustrating activity than trying to reason with an individual in the throes of a romantic love experience. No matter how skillfully rational arguments are marshalled to indicate the inappropriateness

and inadvisability of the romantic choice, it has no apparent effect. Normal reasoning processes seem to have ceased functioning; the lover is untouched by any argument and apparently only concerned about how he feels. He will resist the finest logic with the statement, "I love her." Reasoning is eclipsed by emotion.

In many ways Peter Abelard (1079–1142) represents the blossoming of the intellectual forces leading Europe out of the ignorance and superstition of the Dark Ages. As a brilliant young aristocrat of Breton in the days when the nobility of Europe were turning aside from war and conflict as an outlet for their abundant energies and embarking on a search for knowledge, he joined in the trek from teacher to teacher. His incisive intellect soon challenged his teachers. He debated and defeated William of Champeaux in philosophy. Moving to Laon, he challenged the celebrated theologian Anselm, and without special study or previous training, vanquished him in debate.

Abelard set up his own school and became an outstanding personality of the emerging academic world. By 1115 he had reached the height of his power. Appointed canon and master of Notre Dame, the fame of his learning spread so wide that students flocked to sit at his feet and marvel at his lectures. Few teachers ever held the sway and influence of Abelard.

Abelard boasts, and the correspondence of Héloïse confirms, that not only throngs of students but noble ladies flocked to his lectures. In the midst of all this adulation, one woman, Héloïse, neice of Fulbert, canon of Notre Dame Cathedral, captured his attention. Attractive in appearance, with a keen and inquiring mind, Héloïse presented a challenge to Abelard, who despite his commitment to celibacy in hope of church preferment, determined to win her love.

By flattering Héloïse's uncle and appealing to his greed,

Abelard wormed his way into the house as a boarder and resident teacher, with the strict admonition of the ambitious uncle that he should spend as much time, "day and night" as he could, teaching Héloïse. Abelard took the request rather literally, and it wasn't long before he and Héloïse were busy with extracurricular activities as he became her lover. Smitten, he neglected his lecturing, dismissing his students so that he might spend his time singing the love songs which were echoed and transmitted by the troubadours.

The image of Abelard, the great scholar and intellect of his day, mooning around at the age of forty like a sick calf, is typical of romantic love. He cannot concentrate on his work, sits and sings songs and generally makes a pathetic figure as he is "in love."

Many modern critics have concluded that the value of Abelard's work lay in his emphasis on the importance of a rational presentation of ecclesiastical doctrine. He is said by some to have been the greatest intellect of his day. As a founder of the university movement he fought for the preeminence of reason and its place in religion. Nevertheless, in this episode of his life he is seen with his intellectual capacities altogether subordinated to his emotions.

In the throes of romantic love, reason evaporates as water before the midday sun, and emotion takes over. Its reign is complete.

(5) *The experience of romantic love is often most irrational.* The extravagances of the Minnesinger movement often gave rise to peculiar behavior, and this is nowhere more dramatically portrayed than in the poetic autobiography of Count Ulrich von Lichtenstein (1200–1276) who grew up from a young lad in the sentiments of "lady service" and believed that he should select a lady to serve.

At a tender age he chose a lady already married to another, but waited hopefully for an opportunity to perform some valiant feat for her. In one early moving experience, while serving her as a youthful page, he carefully planned for the moment and rejoiced in the privilege of being able to drink the water in which his lady love had washed her hands.

As he grew, he became aware of his lack of attractiveness, a fact to which the lady did not hesitate to call his attention. To improve his appearance he braced himself for the horrors of medieval surgery and had his harelip operated on by a medieval barber.

In the custom of his day, he fought for his lady in many tournaments. On one occasion when the lady heard that Ulrich had lost his finger in combat she was somewhat annoyed to discover the story was not true. She let him know her displeasure. With not a moment's hesitation, Ulrich hacked off his finger and sent the evidence of his love in a special mount and case to his beloved.

This notable affair climaxed itself in an epic journey in which Ulrich rode from Italy to Bohemia, dressed as the goddess Venus and challenging all knights along the route to meet him in battle so that he could prove his love for the lady of his heart.

In an almost incidental footnote to the story, it might be noted that he had a wife and children during a good proportion of this time. These provided for him the consolations of married life, but in accordance with the rules of chivalry, his love had to be reserved for some unobtainable love object.

If a dweller in modern suburbia were to have a neighbor who embarked on half the strange exploits of Ulrich, he would probably call the police, sympathize with the man's wife and work with relatives to gain at least a temporary commitment for psychiatric care for the individual thus afflicted; but to the followers of romantic love, this kind of behavior was all explicable and understandable.

(6) *The experience of love may immobilize the "victim."*

He met her at a ball in the midst of all the pageantry of the eighteenth century; immediately he was swept away with her simple beauty, and he bent every effort to ascertain more about her. To his delight he discovered she was from a noble family and married to a wealthy old man who had grandchildren older than the youthful wife.

His interest mounted, and he penned an impassioned letter to her, "I had eyes only for you, I admired only you, and longed to be with you alone. Send me an answer quickly, in order that the fire which is consuming me may be appeased."

The lady didn't even condescend to answer, so he wrote again, "Have I displeased you? My passion grows. You rob me of my rest. Vouchsafe a little joy, a little happiness, to the poor heart that would fain worship you. Is it so hard to give me an answer?"

There was yet a third letter of love. So great was his anguish that his emotions were in unimaginable turmoil.

Who is this love-sick Galahad? Is it a poet, a smitten adolescent, or a fawning follower of the foibles of courtly love? No. It is Napoleon Bonaparte, emperor of France, a child of the enlightened scientific age of French culture, who has chilled the hearts of European statesmen with his voracious appetite for conquest.

Thirty-seven years of age and married to Josephine, the object of an earlier love passion, in the midst of a campaign, the sight of Countess Waleska in Poland caused him to "fall in love." His whole life came to a standstill. Moody and irascible, he wandered through the castle where he was in temporary residence. The secretaries, usually busy with a thousand tasks, were dismissed; he refused to confer with his generals; turned away important national delegations; he wouldn't even mount his horses. All of Europe and his cherished schemes had to wait while he worked out his spell of lovesickness.

And Napoleon's experiences are repeated today with monotonous regularity as all sorts of strange behavior are blamed on "love." It is frequently a debilitating experience which lays its victims low, not unlike a spell of illness that puts the patient to bed and for a limited time removes him from his normal activities.

(7) *A lover may be so preoccupied with thoughts of his beloved that the state could only be adequately described as an obsession.* In the neurotic state known as the obsessive compulsive reaction, the victim is plagued by thoughts which cannot be dispelled, or by the compulsion to perform certain irrational acts. In the obsessive aspect, sometimes a thought or an idea cannot be dismissed from the mind. Most people have had the experience of having a tune run through their minds which was almost impossible to reject. A theological student was plagued with the thought to "rape God." The obsession became so overpowering that he could not continue his studies.

The compulsion aspect of the experience may take the form of an urge to perform an apparently meaningless act such as washing one's hands or carrying out some strange, unreasonable ritual.

Romantic love frequently has strong obsessive compulsive overtones. Mr. Seivers, a fifty-year-old man, had five children ranging in ages from seven through eighteen years. His eighteen-year-old daughter, Anne, became friendly with Barbara, a girl of her own age. Anne took Barbara home during school vacation, and the father could not take his eyes off his daughter's girl friend. On several occasions he left his work and traveled two hundred miles on a bus to the town where Barbara and Anne attended school. Ostensibly going to visit Anne, he spent all his time paying attention to the embarrassed Barbara, who complained to his daughter.

Confronted with the situation upon his return, he could

offer no explanation except that he had to see Barbara. Periodically he wrote long letters to her which she immediately
passed on to his daughter. Mr. Seivers gave all the appearance
of being quite helpless in the situation and going through his
behavior even though it was illogical, self-defeating and humil-
iating in its outcome. Rebukes from his frustrated wife only
served to compound the difficulty.

It was apparently ever thus. Some recently discovered trial
records tell the startling story of Sister Virginia, a nun of
Monza who lived in the sixteenth century and entered a
convent when she was fourteen years of age. After seven
uneventful years, when she was twenty-two, Virginia chanced
to look out the nunnery window where she saw Gian Paolo
Osio, a young man of bad reputation, who lived on the estate
close by the nunnery. Sister Virginia tells of her experience,
"After I had seen Osio twice, it seemed as though I were
forced by the devil to go to that window." Thus began one of
the strangest and most sordid love affairs of the seventeenth
century. The nun's feeling of compulsion is typical of much
romantic love.

(8) There are evidences of a well-formed delusional system
in some romantic love encounters. People "in love" will often
build a well-formed delusional system around the object of
their affection. Sydney Harris, a quiet, retiring student, had a
mediocre scholastic record. His hard-working, intelligent wife
determined to motivate her husband to make a success out of
life.

John and Phyllis Stark lived nearby in the student village,
attended the same church, and a friendship developed between the two couples. The moderately attractive Mrs. Stark
fascinated the demure Sydney Harris. As the two couples went
places together, Sydney made it his business to keep close to
Phyllis Stark. He uttered never a word nor did she, but he

received a thousand unspoken messages from her. The way in which she welcomed him when he visited the house or laughed at his feeble efforts at joking all spoke volumes.

On one occasion as they walked down the narrow hallway of the house, he felt her brush herself against him. Another night the two couples met at the Starks before leaving for a party. After joining the other three in the room, Phyllis Stark raised her skirt and straightened her stocking. Sydney immediately got the message that Phyllis was issuing an invitation for a sexual encounter.

Carefully planning his strategy, Sydney dropped in on the Stark household when Johnny was at work. Phyllis welcomed him, and he mustered up enough courage to seize hold of her and pour out his avowals of love. Phyllis was not only unresponsive, she was shocked and scared by the demure one's surge of ardor. She pushed him out of the house, called her husband home, and told her story.

Fortunately the Starks took a sensible view of the whole affair and decided to say nothing to Sydney's wife, and all concerned went to see a marriage counselor.

Mr. Stark was amused by the experience and in no way threatened by the rival for his wife's affections. Mrs. Stark confessed to a feeling of pity for Sydney but denied any romantic inclinations and was horrified at his interpretation of her actions. Sydney, somewhat scared, could only abjectly confess he had been, and still was, in love with Mrs. Stark, that he couldn't live without her; and although she had never said anything, he was still convinced she had given him a hundred signs of encouragement.

After a number of counseling sessions, the counselor was firmly convinced Mrs. Stark was telling the truth. Sydney Harris, overshadowed at home by his efficient wife, dreamed of himself as the great lover and had built up a delusional system in which he played the Casanova role; no amount of counseling was going to deprive him of his delusion.

This survey of characteristics of the varieties of love experiences raises the possibility that love may in reality be a syndrome, a word defined by the dictionary as "the pattern of symptoms that characterize a particular disorder or disease." In this sense we have been spending our time examining a group of symptomatic manifestations which may be indications of an underlying mental disorder.

Lest the investigator feel he has made some startling modern discovery, it might be well to note that the idea is not really new; the Greeks, who made the earliest known efforts to classify mental illness, included a category, "divine madness," and a subclassification, "erotic madness—inspired by Aphrodite and Eros." Periodically the idea reappeared, and in the various classification of illness that of "love sickness" was frequently used. When William Cullen in the eighteenth century made some sort of psychiatric history by coining the term "neurosis," he listed other illnesses which included, "melancholy with violent love."

It doesn't take a very active imagination to see some of the characteristics of romantic love—obsessions, delusional patterns, manic depressive emotional swings—which would lead us to consider we are dealing with an insanity called love.

8

The Rise and Fall of Love

How did man ever get himself into all this confusion about love? One particularly widely accepted explanation is the Marxian formulation that the concept of love may be nothing more than a reflection of the mode of economic production and exchange. With the emergence of the idea of private property, there came the desire for exclusive possession of a spouse.

For a closed society the possibilities that such an intimate matter as the individual's love life is amenable to control has had a certain appeal. News out of North Vietnam tells of the slogan of "Three Postponements." If you are single, postpone falling in love. If you are in love, postpone marriage. If married, postpone having children. Love, marriage, children—all these experiences must not interfere with the nation's war effort. The welfare of the country comes before the individual's personal desires.

All of this has led to the idea that it is possible to tell a man's nationality by the way he reacts to meeting a woman. An Englishman shakes hands; an American asks her for a date; a Frenchman kisses her; a Russian cables Moscow for instructions.

All of this is a far cry from capitalist America where almost any behavior can be justified by saying, "we are in love," and indolent hippies wishing to withdraw from society proclaim themselves "love children" while holding out a begging hand for welfare checks.

The news from some Communist countries that the faithful party die-hards are now saying, "sex is the opiate of the masses," may indicate some of the difficulties they have encountered in controlling this powerful reaction in human personality. From this perspective love may even be seen as a capitalist plot to subvert the proletariat and drain away their enthusiasm for a drab society in which all people are equal but some more equal than others. However, any unbiased observer knows love is far too complex an experience to be explained in this way.

After perusing the previous chapter, the reader easily gets the idea that the insanity called love, which overtakes a goodly proportion of the population, leaves its subject like hit-and-run victims strewn along life's pathway, in an abnormal and emotionally incapacitated condition. However, if we review the series of presentations in the earlier chapters other and more positive characteristics become evident.

Even romantic love itself has brought a number of positive values to men and women and society in general. An examination of the courtly love of Eleanor's day shows us some of the values which emerged.

(1) Courtly love brought a new image of womanhood. Before the advent of courtly love, a woman was just another of

the lord's possessions along with his estates, cattle and serfs. The main differentiating factor was that she had the advantage of bringing new domains with her, and it was often said that when the feudal lord decided on matrimony he married a "fief," or feudal estate, just as if the estates were the main gain, with the wife thrown in as a sort of a bonus premium. Her main function on assuming her position was to provide the lord with offspring. Just as his cattle bred and enlarged his herds, he needed a wife who could provide the heirs so vital under the feudal system. Possibly the most important reason given for the king of France's divorce of Eleanor of Acquitaine was that she had not produced a male heir.

The lord of the manor had the power to determine that the widow of his vassal remarried the proper person. Later the arrangement was made a little more flexible and the widow could pay a fee to gain her independence. One entry in the English exchequer rolls states, "Alice, Countess of Warwick, renders account of 100 and five palfreys, to be allowed to remain a widow as long as she pleases and not be forced to marry by the king." The inferior woman was at the disposal of her lord.

Courtly love brought the new emphasis that women were to be wooed, won, and pleased. The knight was the champion of God and the ladies. From being the temptress who lured him to destruction she now became his inspirer and guiding star. The lover must be willing to serve his beloved under any circumstances and obey her wishes and commands. The crusades were ventures of knightly courage upon which many a man embarked to show his chivalrous spirit, but they brought a secondary gain for women. While the lord was away crusading, his lady often stepped up to new responsibilities in running the affairs of the castle and gained a new status.

Courtly love started a revolution in the status of women.

The process of placing woman on a pedestal had begun; and whatever we might think of the outcome, the new position was superior to the bottomless pit to which the Church had assigned her, or the castle prison of the Dark Ages. Women would never again return to the status they had occupied before Eleanor's day.

(2) Courtly love put sex in a new perspective. Although it has been seen as adulterous by many writers, the adultery of courtly love must be considered against the background of the feudal practice of marriage as a means of joining estates or kingdoms. Courtly love emphasized the personal attraction for man and woman to each other.

Sex had been a biological function to gain release for the man or propagate children. Now came an idea of the fidelity of one man to one woman even without sexual relations.

One group of historians maintains that the ideal love affair in courtly love is never consummated. The man is forever struggling for the woman; and when she deigns to favor him, it is a long-drawn-out "petting" period which always stops short of consummation. If they "go all the way," it is frequently spoken of as "mixed love."

There is never just a straight, direct approach to sexual relations. The whole atmosphere surrounding the sexual relationship has been changed.

(3) From courtly love there emanated an entirely new note to permeate all society. The crudity and coarseness of the life of the Middle Ages is beyond the imaginings of modern man. In the castle, which was the height of society, the table leftovers were flung to the omnipresent dogs and left with the dog dung until the smell became intolerable. For a plate each couple had a round, thick piece of wood called a trencher. The food was placed on the trencher; and after the meal eaten by the diner, given to the dogs swarming around, or sent to the

poor. Two people often shared the same wooden cup; forks were known in the 13th century but seldom provided; and each diner used his own knife to hack off his meat.

Cleanliness was not next to godliness; the monks of the early Church had set an example of refraining from washing. In England it was not until 1254 when, significantly enough, it was Eleanor of Castile arriving from Spain to become the bride of the future Edward I who had her servants spread carpets on the floor of her apartment after the Spanish custom. From this beginning the custom spread throughout England.

The new emphasis focused on courtesy, good manners, devotion, and self-denial. Knights went off on strange and apparently ridiculous enterprises to impress their lady loves, yet there was associated with all this the idea that the knight had to prove himself worthy, improve himself, and be willing to sacrifice that he might fulfill his obligations.

Despite these gains romantic love by its very nature is impermanent, transitory, and fitful. As Johnson said it, "The feeling of friendship is like being comfortably full of roast beef; love like being enlived with champaign." And who wants to spend life in a sea of bubbly effervescence? The Greeks with their precise language used another word. While *eros* described the more emotional type of experience, *philia* was used to indicate the more rational reactions of shared interests which form the basis of a lasting relationship.

The highly romantic Disraeli found his most satisfying experiences with a tastelessly dressed older woman given to making shocking faux pas. Yet Mary Ann, doting on him, fussing like a hen round her chick, anticipating his needs and hanging on every word, provided just the stimulus he needed to fulfill his role in British politics.

Luther's marriage had none of the usual overtones of romantic love. He simply assumed his responsibility. It was of the same order as that of Calvin who asked his friends to select a bride for him. Far from the romantic love which seeks the exclusive possession of the love object Luther's moved out in ever-widening circles—Katie, children, relatives, boarders. Its socializing processes provided experiences which helped the reformer to develop his potential and set a pattern for family life.

John Wesley's unfortunate love affairs dramatized the struggle of a man who could never quite properly relate a love for God and women. The earnest minded Puritan felt women might interfere with his quest for God and service to his fellow man. In the tragedy of his disappointing love experiences, he discovered a new dimension of service both to God and to his fellow man.

Love is an object relationship; and this is nowhere more clearly demonstrated than in the life and love of David Livingstone. His passion for studying the nature of things—the human body, geology, astronomy, hydraulics, the whole mysterious African continent—coupled with a conviction about the message of the gospel and its civilizing force, and the horrors of slavery which wrenched a man from his home and family and treated him worse than cattle, possessed the soul of Livingstone. Livingstone's experience stands as mute evidence of the number of objects which may be loved by one mortal.

A modern psychology has made us familiar with the term *sublimation* which is used to describe the redirection of a fundamental drive of personality into some new channel. Anton T. Boisen, intelligent, trained in the ideas of twentieth-century social sciences, was caught up in a love affair that tantalized him all his days. Yet in the frustrations of denial, he gave himself over to working for his fellowman in an enterprise which revolutionized the helping ministry of thousands of clergymen. His thwarted love for a woman found expression in a wider love for his fellow man.

In the letters to the Corinthians Christians, themselves a fascinating psychological revelation of Paul's inner turmoil and distress, the apostle sets forth, like a tranquil stream amidst a series of tempestuous waterfalls, a gem of prose unparalleled in ancient or modern literature. His hymn to love (1 Corinthians 13) expounds with lucidity, feeling and inspiration what Henry Drummond calls "the greatest thing in the world," agape love, the third of the Greek triad.

The climactic statement in the heart of the passage is his assertion about agape love or "gift love," in which he says, "Love never fails." Translated "fails" in the King James version, the Greek work ekpipto used in the statement can be variously rendered. It is used to describe a ship off its course, a star falling from heaven, or an actor hissed off stage. The most widely used metaphor is the process of fading, so often utilized in the Old Testament as when Isaiah says, "We all do fade as a leaf," describing the process of deterioration. Arthur S. Way tries to catch the force of the figure in his translation, "Love's flower petals never fall." [1] Love knows no autumn; it is perpetually spring, with no deterioration but continuing to blossom in the evergreen wonder of its constancy.

As important as is the receiving of love, it shrinks into insignificance in the total love experience; for the pathway is from self to others, from receiving to giving. Under the influence of love, the personality unfolds and expands; but then like the baby who having grown to adulthood begets children of his own, so the mature person inevitably moves out from being loved to take initiative in loving and in turn providing for others that which was so essential in his own experience.

Love is the most creative of all the emotions. Anger, envy, resentment, are primitive responses which, like a fierce tornado funnelling down with indiscriminate and capricious power, are blindly and illogically bent on the expression of hostility, leaving destruction in their wake. The great anatomist John Hunter, is reputed to have said concerning his heart condition, "My life is at the mercy of any rascal who can make me angry." Negative emotions, Samson-like, not only tear down the structure of human relationships but destroy the subject himself in the collapse. By contrast the positive power of love brings out life's healing potential.

Because of its pervading power, love is the supreme activity of the human personality. Paul says, ". . . whether there be prophecies, they shall fail; whether there be tongues, they shall cease; whether there be knowledge, it shall vanish away. . . . love never fades." One by one the coveted gifts of ministry, prophecy, tongues, and knowledge will fulfill their purpose and cease to be, but love continues unabated as the immortal aspect of personality.

Referring to the feats of the Roman soldiers who in addition to their practiced skill with arms, took spade and pick-axe to construct the fortifications of their camps, Gibbon says, "Active valour may often be the present of nature; but such patient diligence can be the fruit only of habit and discipline." The progress of the development of agape love is on something of the same order. The eros encounter is exciting, with racing pulse and palpitating heart, but agape is the long steady haul characterized by perseverance and persistency. It is not an inherited capacity but rather the fruit of long and patient discipline.

Drummond exhorts his readers to note the way of learning to love:

What makes a man a good cricketer: Practice. What makes a man a good artist, a good sculptor, a good musician? Practice. What makes a man a good linguist, a good stenographer? Practice.

What makes a man a good man? Practice. Nothing else. . . . Love is not a thing of enthusiastic emotion. It is a rich, strong, manly, vigorous expression of the whole round Christian character—the Christlike nature in its fullest development. And the constituents of this great character are only to be built up by ceaseless practice.[2]

Although sometimes written about with sickly sentimentality, there is really no place for theoretical "eggheads" in the process of agape love. It is only developed in the school of life with constant and diligent involvement in the experience of loving.

Agape or giving love has been expounded with great clarity by Pitirim A. Sorokin, whose personal experiences could hardly seem less likely to convince a man of the power of altruistic love.

A leading Russian intellectual, Sorokin was not sorry to see the overthrow of the backward Tzarist regime and worked as secretary to Kerensky, the leader of the provisional government. After the Bolsheviks had displaced the elected representatives of the people by force of arms and assumed control, Sorokin became an object of their antagonism. Hounded down and imprisoned, he lived in daily expectancy of death, watching his fellow prisoners taken away to be shot.

In the midst of all these horrors, Sorokin sat down to make notable entry in his diary. He concluded that his nightmarish experience had taught him three great lessons. (1) Life even at its worst and hardest was the most beautiful, wonderful, miraculous treasure in all the world. (2) The fulfillment of duty is the response that makes life happy. (3) It is utterly futile to try to create a new world through cruelty, hatred, violence, and injustice. The only way is through creative love not only preached but constantly practiced.

It is small wonder Sorokin had dedicated himself to the propagation of his idea of altruistic love.

The Apostle John, a "Son of Thunder," who with righteous

indignation demanded that Jesus call down fire on an unresponsive village, later became the apostle of love. The passing years in the Christian fellowship had brought about a change and a mellowing process. In old age, grown feeble and weak, he was carried to the gatherings of the church where instead of a formal discourse he simply said, "Little children, love one another."

Concerned with the monotonous repetition of this admonition, some of the elders asked, "Master, why dost thou always say this?"

The aged apostle replied, "It is the Lord's command, and if this alone is done it is enough."

The world needs more lovers! The great lovers of the world are not Casanova, Don Juan, or even Elizabeth Taylor, but rather Francis of Assisi, Albert Schweitzer, or Lottie Moon, whose interest reached to all humanity.

We can only learn to love as we love. The activity breeds the skill, and no better starting point could be made than by reading and putting into practice Paul's great hymn to love, 1 Corinthians 13, and by finally concluding with him, "And now abideth faith, hope, love, these three, but the greatest of these is love."

REFERENCES

Chapter 1

1. Amy Kelly, *Eleanor of Aquitaine and the Four Kings* (Cambridge: Harvard University Press, 1950), p. 24.
2. Ibid., p. 61.
3. Ibid., p. 245.
4. Ibid., p. 162.

Chapter 2

1. Preserved Smith and Charles Jacobs (eds.), *Luther's Correspondence and Other Contemporary Letters* (Philadelphia: Lutheran Publication Society, 1913–18), 2, 258. Cited in William H. Lazareth, *Luther on the Christian Home* (Philadelphia: Muhlenberg Press, 1960), p. 18.
2. Lazareth, p. 9.
3. Ibid., p. 34.
4. Preserved Smith, *The Life and Letters of Martin Luther* (Boston: Houghton Mifflin, 1911), p. 168. Cited in Lazareth, *Luther on the Christian Home*, p. 23.
5. Roland H. Bainton, *Here I Stand* (Nashville: Abingdon Press, 1950), p. 295.
6. Lazareth, *Luther in the Christian Home*, p. 226.
7. Ibid., p. 31.
8. Ibid., p. 29.
9. Erik H. Erikson, *Young Man Luther* (New York: W. W. Norton & Company, Inc., 1958), p. 233.
10. Lazareth, p. 234.

Chapter 3

1. *The Book of Common Prayer* . . . according to the use of The Church of England (London: Cambridge University Press), p. 257.

Chapter 5

1. David Chamberlin, *Some Letters From Livingstone* (London: Oxford University Press, 1940), pp. 1–2.
2. W. Gordon Blaikie, *The Personal Life of David Livingstone* (New York: Fleming H. Revell Company, 1880), p. 86.
3. George Seaver, *David Livingstone: His Life and Letters* (New York: Harper & Brothers, 1957), p. 85.
4. Blaikie, p. 87.
5. Seaver, p. 86.
6. Blaikie, p. 122.
7. Ibid., p. 147.
8. Ibid., p. 155.
9. Ibid., p. 216.
10. Ibid., p. 221–22.
11. Seaver, p. 294.
12. Blaikie, pp. 254–55.
13. Ibid., p. 412.

Chapter 8

1. Arthur S. Way, *The Letters of Saint Paul* (Chicago: Moody Press, 1950).
2. Henry Drummond, *The Greatest Thing in the World* (Old Tappan, N.J.: Fleming H. Revell Co., Inspirational Classics Series), pp. 42–43.